Expect the Unexpected!

The memoirs of a suburban educator in California

BY

LEE WILDES

PAGE PUBLISHING, INC.
New York, NY

First originally published by Page Publishing, Inc. 2015

ISBN 978-1-68213-229-6 (pbk)
ISBN 978-1-68213-230-2 (digital)

Printed in the United States of America

Introduction

My name is *not* Lee Wildes. I chose this *nom de plume* from a combination of family names and to avoid any personal conflicts that might evolve from the reading of the text. The names of the teachers, administrators, and students are all fictional throughout this memoir and were changed to avoid any negative repercussions. The events depicted are all true to the best of my recollection. The name of the area is also fictional and all historical references discussed in each chapter are generally true with regard to historical records. However, the physical descriptions of the area are quite accurate. Many people who live in California could probably identify similar features and might consider that I was relating to their communities. All the schools mentioned in this memoir are fictitious except one whose name could not possibly be made up, but that will be obvious when you read the text.

This is not a critique of public education in the State of California, but an attempt to reflect on my own perceptions, observations, and attitudes that I have developed over my career. I wrote this memoir to entertain, inform, and perhaps, to enlighten the readers about what it was like to teach social studies in a suburban and affluent community over a forty-plus year span of time.

I did not create a chronological text but chose to develop topics that I thought were both interesting and provocative. I hope the reader will keep an open mind and not be too judgmental in assessing both my actions as a teacher or my style of writing.

CHAPTER I

Environmental Setting

In the early 1960s, Starr Valley was a small village hidden between two branches of the coastal range of California. The valley itself was mostly farmland and livestock ranches. Most visitors who came through the valley during this time would call the area peaceful and even bucolic. There was only one two-lane highway that ran through the valley with some connecting roads that wound through the hills to other valleys. The climate was ideal for most people. It was hot in the summer with temperatures hovering from 90 up to 110 degrees Fahrenheit on particularly hot days. Spring and fall had the best weather patterns of the year as the temperature rarely went over 85°F. or under 60°F. Winter was always chancy because of Thule fog. California, especially the central valley, has a winter time pattern of ground-hugging fog that usually comes after a big rainstorm. Some days the fog does not lift until there are either off-shore or northern winds clearing the air. These days tend to be very depressing and have a negative effect on the mood of the people. For the most part the weather patterns don't change much year after year. This may be one of the reasons for the large influx of suburban sprawl that took place over the next forty years.

The hills surrounding the valley are green in the winter and early spring but become brown the rest of the year. The largest mountain in the foothills was to the east of the valley. It was named Mt. Delgado after a Spanish conquistador who during the early 1700s climbed to the top and proclaimed the whole area for Spain. He settled for the eastern part of the mountain because of an ongoing conflict with the Native Americans who inhabited the valley and western foothills. What happened to the Native Americans who resided in the area is a mystery. Some historians thought that they all died out because of disease; others contend that the Spanish finally defeated them and drove them off the land in the late 1700s; still others, contend that the original white settlers killed them all off in the 1800s. By the twentieth century, the valley was dominated by apple, pear, peach, and walnut orchards owned by white farmers who made a comfortable, but not affluent, living up until the 1960s. The residents who moved into the area during the post–World War II years liked the climate and its relative remoteness from the hectic pace of life found in most metropolitan areas.

By the 1960s, most of the homes in the valley tended to be on the expensive side and this pattern was to continue for the next forty plus years. The most expensive homes were on the hills surrounding the valley where doctors, lawyers, and successful CEOs lived. Many of them commuted to their respective jobs in nearby metropolitan areas, traveling approximately twenty miles each way. There were only a few housing developments on the valley floor with one being a country club for the upper middle and upper class inhabitants of the area. Within the country club, the houses and adjacent properties tended to run from at least $80,000 up to $200,000, which was considered expensive in the 1960s. Today, none of these homes would sell for less than $1,000,000. The other housing developments were built to accommodate middle to lower middle-class families and were in close proximity to the village stores. Those houses sold for prices that ranged between $12,000 and $35,000. Again, these same houses today would not sell for less than $600,000. In the 1960s, housing developments were not necessarily noticeable to most of the casual visitors passing through the valley because they were generally hidden behind the groves of trees, which dominated the valley, and the area was not considered to be anything more than rural farmland. The farmers and ranchers who lived in the valley and surrounding hills were to become more affluent in the ensuing years from the sale of land to real estate developers, high tech industries, and shopping centers. The commuters who established residences were mostly wealthy, white, protestant, Anglo-Saxons who eschewed living among minorities in nearby metropolitan areas. As the 1960s saw substantial changes in the social atmosphere of the United States, many white families took flight to rural areas to escape the anxiety of the Civil Rights movement, the protests against the Vietnam War, and the growing counter-culture revolution taking place in large urban areas of the United States. In the early 1960s, the United States Government set up an ultra-secret weapons lab about twenty miles to the east and thus placed the valley midway between the lab and university facilities located twenty miles to the west. This had a significant influence on the demographics of the valley as scientists and technicians moved into the valley and mostly worked at both facilities. This influx of these "newcomers" was to have a profound effect on future decades of development in the valley and especially the school system.

The village, itself, had been in existence for over a century. It was developed by a frontiersman named Charles Starr who gained the land through some questionable dealings with the Mexican government during the Bear Flag Revolt in the 1840s. It was a stage-coach stop during the 1850s and had one hotel that served guests until World War II. By the early 1960s, the population was no more than about twelve thousand residents. The hotel then became a landmark and served as a restaurant with a bar and had novelty shops in areas once occupied by guests. The valley had only one high school, a junior high (seventh and eighth grades), and three or four elementary schools. The village had two or three gas stations, a series of small mom and pop stores that served the area for more than sixty years. It had one dairy fountain where one could get milkshakes, sandwiches, and light fare. There was one other bar that had steady customers for most of the century and became the favorite spot for the farmers and ranchers on Friday nights. Later on it became the Friday afternoon "watering hole" for the local teachers trying to make sense of the rigors of the week and lamenting the reasons for getting into education when so many of their college friends were making more money. I was one of them! But before I delve into my career of more than forty years trying to educate American youth, I want to establish the atmosphere, attitudes, and environment that existed in the valley during the early 1960s.

CHAPTER 2

The Social Setting

Up to the early 1960s, the valley was mostly inhabited by WASP residents who were very conservative and had sharply-defined opinions on virtually every controversial issue that defined the 1960s. If liberals existed among the power elite of the valley, they remained silent and non-confrontational. School board meetings were not too exciting (they never are) because everyone seemed to hold the same views and no one expressed a dissenting opinion. Teachers felt that they had to come to the meetings with bowed heads and demonstrable, submissive gestures. Raises were not readily forthcoming and the prevailing feeling among many of the teachers was that the relationship between the school board and the teachers was something akin to a feudal, lord-serf relationship. Any union activity was greatly frowned upon. The local PTA was dominated by middle-age matrons who had a well-established "pecking order." The longer residing members with the most income tended to dominate all meetings. In my first year of teaching, I would always run into the president of the PTA when I was coming out of a store with a six-pack of beer or a fifth of hard liquor. She seemed to be hiding in the bushes waiting for me.

She would always say, "Well hello, Mr. Wildes! I see that you are busy shopping for the necessities of life!" She always had this disapproving and disdainful tone of voice. I am surprised that she didn't try to have me fired as a hopeless alcoholic and a bad influence on American youth. I, also, believe that my manner of dress had something to do with her attitude. On the weekends, I seldom shaved and walked around with flip-flop sandals. I am sure my image was not considered in anyway conducive to setting the proper example for the children of the valley. After a few months, I took to wearing sport coats, slacks, and shoes while carrying large shopping bags where the contents were not available to prying eyes. But even this seemed not enough to dispel the suspicions and scrutiny of the "alpha female" of the PTA.

In the early 1960s, there was a group of hard-core reactionaries who viewed dissent with suspicion and as a product of communist subversion. They were collectively known as the John Birch Society. John Birch was reputedly a government agent who was captured, tortured, and killed by the Chinese Communists in the late 1940s. He became a hero and idol of the post-McCarthy, anti-Communist factions of the late 1950s and early 1960s. Starr Valley had one of the most vocal groups of "Birchers" in California. High school teachers were constantly scrutinized by this group for what we taught in our classes. Textbooks were constantly being attacked for any divergent views that could be construed as being written by "Reds" or "Pinkos." "Reds" were die-hard, card-carrying members of the American Communist Party. Since the McCarthy era did not provide evidence of Communist infiltration into various segments of American society, the "Birchers" launched into the "Pinko" campaign. A "Pinko" was one who was sympathetic to left-wing programs labeled as Communist-inspired and was, therefore, guilty by association. One of our teachers, whose name was Ivan Molensk, was a grandson of Russian émigrés who came to the United States during one of the Czar's pograms of the nineteenth century. He was educated at the state university in a nearby metropolitan area and was constantly harassed because of his college associations and the fact that his relatives came from Russia. Whenever Ivan would lecture to the classes there was always a student who taped the lecture and took it home. We normally gave permission to students who had problems listening or taking notes and allowed them to record the lecture providing they asked permission. However, there was one case in which a student taped his lecture, took it home, and either he or his parents had re-recorded the lecture with key points left out. The modified tape was sealed in a manila envelop and sent to the principal without any name on it from the sender. The principal, at least, called in our team to listen to what was recorded. After listening to it, we came to the conclusion that the student or his parents were trying to stir up trouble. The matter was dropped after we were in unanimous agreement that the recording was modified to cast doubts upon the loyalty of Ivan. One member of the John Birch Society went so far as to infiltrate a party held in a public restaurant twenty miles away to honor a retiring Political Science professor from the local college. The professor wrote books regarding the hysteria, "witch hunts" and paranoia of the post–World War II era, and he steadfastly criticized the "red-baiting" that had gone on in Washington during the early 1950s. The infiltrator was specifically shadowing Ivan to gain incriminating evidence of his political leanings and associations. He clandestinely took a series of pictures of the social contacts made during the affair with the intention of influencing the school board to have him fired. The pictures showed up at school board meeting with the infiltrator demanding action toward dismissal. Ivan was not invited to the meeting and heard about the accusations the next day. Fortunately, most members of the school board dismissed the claims as products of prejudice and hysteria and the matter was dropped. Ivan considered suing the culprit, but decided that it would not be in his best interest.

In the late 1960s, a National League baseball star bought a home in the wealthier part of Starr Valley and was prepared to move into his new residence when some neighbors found out that he was black. They initiated a petition to nullify the sale of the property, claiming that the valley was not place for minorities and that his presence would bring down property values. The petition was signed by 80 percent of the residents living on the same street. Many of the teachers at Starr Valley High School organized a demonstration on his behalf. While the moving vans were unloading his furniture, a group of racists donned white sheets and made a series of threats to his family and the teachers who supported him. Since this was the middle of baseball season, the star athlete was not present when all this transpired. The confrontation became quite heated and one of the teachers got into fight with the protesters. Someone called the county sheriff's office. Unfortunately, their presence did little to reduce the tension and hostility that broke out. Because of the growing conflict and the little attention given to the warnings by one of the deputy sheriffs, there was a need to call in for more police reinforcements. Things got out of hand when rocks were thrown into the crowd of defenders. One of the teachers was injured and had to be taken to the local hospital for treatment. When one of the rock throwers was handcuffed and taken away, the crowd grew increasingly hostile. The police were forced to use tear gas to breakup the protesting crowd as the number of people supporting the residents grew. With the increasing presence of local police, deputy sheriffs, and members of the California Highway Patrol the hostility subsided and many of the protesters left the scene. That night some of the protesters had painted epithets on the garage door and front walkway of the house. A series of warnings about burnings and violence toward the family prompted the law enforcement agencies to post a twenty-four-hour guard on the home. The baseball player's family decided that it was not safe, even with a police guard, and left to stay with relatives outside of the area. When the police guard withdrew, someone attempted to burn down the home. The damage was not too extensive, but the family never returned. When baseball season ended, the baseball star took legal action and managed, after a couple of years, to regain all his investment back.

Outside of the person who was handcuffed, no one was arrested, and the perpetrator was released with nothing more than a warning. The teacher who was injured had some stitches and returned to work the next day. Whoever threw the rock that hit him was never brought to justice. Shortly afterwards, the Rumpford Fair Housing Act was passed. It attempted to outlaw discrimination in real estate transactions, but it came too late for this family.

In the late 1980s, there was a different, almost comical, protest that evolved in the valley.

There was a street called Gay Lane. It had that name long before I came to work in the local high school. It was named after a student that I had in American government during my first year of teaching. There were only two houses on the street at that time. The street was named by the grandfather to honor his firstborn grandchild. He apparently owned all the land around the area and had Gay and her parents move into the second house that was built there. For the next twenty to thirty years, all the properties were sold and houses were built on them. In the late 1980s, a person who was interested in buying one of the houses from the owners objected to the name of the street and before it closed escrow managed to circulate a petition to rename the street because he didn't want to give out his address to his friends and business associates with the name Gay on it. The grandfather had passed on and Gay had married and moved out of the area. The new owner apparently had success in getting a majority of the residents to sign the petition and he presented it to the City Planning Commission. Word got out that they were considering changing the name when a news program from one of the surrounding cities decided to feature it on the evening news. The next day a group of supporters for the Gay Liberation Movement had organized a protest and sit-in to block all access in and out of the street. The residents rose up and threatened this group of protesters with violence. The Gay Liberation Movement even brought the matter at the next City Council meeting. During the meeting, no one understood the origin of the name. Apparently, the residents who lived on the street did not know the history of the area and didn't know of its origin. Someone made a comment to the extent that there must have been some homosexuals living in the area when development began. I read all about it in the local newspaper and thought it was humorous. However, members of the community were divided and accusations and threats came from both sides. The Gay Liberation Movement did not give up easily and managed to get legal advice to stop the renaming. After a few heated meetings with the city council, the matter was put to a voice vote by its members. There was an on-going threat to have a recall election if any members objected to the renaming. The process dragged on for a month. I finally got tired of hearing all the comments and ignorance regarding the name of the street and called the city manager and explained the history of the name. The matter was brought to a close when a poll of all the residents on the street decided that renaming the street was appropriate. The Gay Liberation Movement threatened further action, but the whole matter was dropped when more serious concerns regarding discrimination drew attention away from the area. The street was renamed "High Street." I was surprised that some one didn't protest that name because of the references to drug use, but nothing occurred.

From the early 1970s until the present, Starr Valley underwent a great transformation as the developers and entrepreneurs moved in like locusts developing the land, establishing high-end housing, promoting shopping centers, and encouraging high-tech firms to establish research and development facilities. The ethnic composition of the area changed also. No longer was the area strictly WASP. Asians, Middle Easterners, and Europeans moved into the area. They were all successful in whatever profession they represented. Mostly they were involved in the high tech industries that came into the valley and their influence upon the educational future of the valley was profound. As a result, the educational curricula changed reflecting the growing emphasis upon higher academic standards and college preparation and less on vocational education. Where some forty years earlier, conservatism was the basic philosophy dominating the politics of the valley; today a greater diversity of opinions and attitudes permeate the intellectual and social environment of the valley. Affluence, however, continued to set the economic climate of the area much to the chagrin of young teachers who came to work in this district. Most could not afford to live in the area and were forced to commute over longer distances.

CHAPTER 3

Institutional Changes

The second high school was built in the late 1960s and was located in the north end of the valley. As more affluent people moved into the valley, there was a need to have two high schools and the north end of the valley became the logical site for the new school. It was appropriately named El Norte High School and virtually all the students who attended the new school came from affluent or very affluent families. While the school was being built, both schools shared the same facilities and the school schedule had to be adjusted to accommodate the large number of students. Some classes began at 7:00 AM and the latest class was scheduled for 4:00 PM. Confusion seemed to be the order of the day as many students thought they were in their own school but ended up in the other school's classes. The first couple of weeks of school were chaotic. I spent more time trying to get the right student into the right class in the right high school. I only hope that when the students got their grades they were a true reflection of their proper assignments. Many of the faculty members had requested to be assigned to the new school and a few of them were confused about what classes they were teaching, when the class was to be held, and, importantly, where the class was being held. I had two class periods in which I almost had to share the same class with a math teacher from the other high school. It took one week to get the problem straightened out. Since it was September, the weather was warm, and for the whole week, I conducted class outside in the lawn area. When the problem was resolved, the students were reluctant to go into a classroom and preferred to stay outdoors. Needless to say, not much learning took place during that week. Luckily, the new high school was finished before winter vacation and the whole school was moved to their location without incident.

In the mid-1970s there was a new high school built in the south end of the valley to accommodate the growth of new students coming into the district. If there was a less expensive area of the valley, it was in the south end. More affordable housing was made available as new tracts of houses were being built. The population density was greater in this area than any other part of the valley and, thus, the need to build a new high school became a top priority. When the high school was about to open there was a contest to name the new school. After about a month, members of the school board had come to the conclusion that Vista Delgado, named after the most prominent peak in the area, was the best entry and upon concluding an open community meeting made the announcement. After the meeting a couple of district administrators and some of the teachers met at a local bar to celebrate the new school's name. After a few drinks, someone called attention to the athletic awards given to deserving athletes at the new high school and questioned whether the parents or the community would approve of student-athletes walking around with VD on their sweaters or jackets. Someone suggested that their mascot should be the crab, and I came up with their school song: "Let's all clap for Vista Delgado!" The next day after an emergency meeting of the school board the name was dropped and a less controversial name was immediately adopted. It became known as El Sud High School.

The number of schools in the whole district has quadrupled over these decades and where there was only one high school in the early sixties, there are four today. If one were to come back to this valley after a forty-year hiatus, he or she would not recognize any of the original landscape and probably would get lost looking for familiar landmarks.

CHAPTER 4

Education as a Career

My career in education began in the fall of 1963. I was one of twenty teachers who were hired during the Summer time. There was one of biggest turnovers in teachers in the school's history. Many of us questioned what happened in the prior year that so many vacancies were created. When asking veteran teachers, we got vague, noncommittal answers; and being new, we decided to drop the inquiry. My job was ideal, as I taught two freshmen (ninth grade) World History classes and three senior (twelfth grade) American Government classes. The World History classes were self-contained classes; while the American Government classes were team taught. Team-teaching was a new force in education during the early 1960s. We had four members who were assigned thirty students each. We would plan all the lessons together, take turns lecturing in a large lecture hall and meet with smaller classes in self-contained classrooms to discuss the lessons, review for exams, and administer tests. For the most part, we would meet in the large lecture hall for lectures, films, guest speakers, and special programs. The success of the team-teaching concept was based upon cooperation among the members, the diversity of teaching styles, and the variable experiences available to the students. I am not sure who got the most from the experience, the new teachers or the students. In any case, the college-level experiences inherent in this program were always rated at the top of the list when graduating students were asked to reflect on their high school years and what were their best classes. It was helpful to cite the evidence from these surveys when other departments on campus were complaining about the team approach to education. Most of the complaints centered on some teachers who would use the faculty room for discussion and preparation. I always felt that there was always a lot of "sour grapes" and jealousy, but the complaints persisted for years.

It is important to look at the faculty in 1963 and the standards they set compared to the influx of newer teachers in the latter part of the 1960s. All the teachers in the high school were white from middle-class backgrounds. All came from respectable colleges and from all indications were competent in subject matter. For the first three years of my career, all the male teachers wore suits and ties. All the women teachers were required to wear dresses, and from any casual observation by outsiders, we reflected the conservative nature of the community. However, in our government classes there was a growing awareness that our clothes and philosophies did not match the standards set by the community. One of the units under study focused on Civil Rights, and we had speakers from both the Ku Klux Klan and the Black Panther organization who came to make separate presentations. We avoided having them on the same day! The speaker from the Klan provided the usual rhetoric and rationale that has dominated much racist thinking since before the American Revolution. He was unwilling to field questions from the audience much to the chagrin of the students who were eager to challenge him on his notions. The Black Panther on the other hand was more than willing to engage in a dialog with the students. Afterwards, the prevailing feeling among most of the students was that the Civil Rights movement had merit and racism had to be eliminated. Some of the students felt, however, that we were pushing the Civil Rights agenda and rejecting the traditional white perspective. As a result, we were all required to attend the next school board meeting and explain our case. After an hour of hearing a diatribe from one of the parent committees, we were allowed to give our case in less than ten minutes. Fortunately, a large number of our students came into the meeting at the last minute and extended the limit for equal time by personally supporting the manner in which we portrayed both sides of the controversy. The board then gave us a reprieve and warned us against having radicals from the Black Panther organization coming on our campus again. Nothing was said about the Ku Klux Klan.

Team teaching was not always mired in controversy. For the most part, we all got along and were very cooperative. When we would set up "point-counterpoint" sessions, we could role-play various political ideologies and could provide provocative and lively discussions. It was fun and engaging for both the students and the teachers. Not all of our activities were serious, and periodically some humor would come into the proceedings. One of our team teachers was in her eighth month of pregnancy and was scheduled to give a lecture on the relations between government and labor. Due to her extreme discomfort, we decided that she should speak from the stage by sitting on a comfortable chair. After we had set the scene for her, she came into the room, sat down, put her arms on her bulging stomach, and proceeded to begin her lecture by stating, "Today, we will be discussing labor movements!" I, unfortunately, addressed one of my colleagues, who was not out of earshot of the audience, that, "I hope none of them take place within the next fifty minutes!" It took about twenty minutes of sincere apologies and attempts to quell the laughter before she could continue with her lecture. Luckily, she laughed along with everyone else but was forced to give an abbreviated version of the lecture. I learned a lesson and tried to keep my comments to myself or at least out of earshot of students.

After teaching American government for two years, I requested to be on the United States History team because I felt more comfortable dealing with the subject matter and

liked their approach to teaching better. I have always had a secret desire to become an actor and was in more than one play in high school and college. Role-playing lends itself to teaching history. Most of the US History team was into assuming the roles of famous persons in American History, and I wanted to be part of the "cast." We structured the team in the same way as American Government. Most of us would dress up in historical costumes, come to class, and either debate or respond to structured questions. The structured questions were prompts made up by the team for our character's views on controversial historical issues. For example, I dressed up and played the role of Andrew Jackson with leather clothes and a coon-skin hat. I had to respond to questions regarding some of the questionable actions he took during his Presidency. One of the questions was, "How could you as President of the United States defy the Supreme Court's decision and force the Cherokee Nation out of their ancestral lands in Georgia?" I won't go into the details, but I had to assume the brash, arrogant, and racial attitudes he displayed during that time period. Students were given the opportunity and were greatly encouraged to ask questions in addition to the provided structured questions. All the teachers played similar roles and we had a lot of fun doing it. During the years we team-taught United States History, I played Alexander Hamilton, his adversary Thomas Jefferson, Andrew Jackson, his adversary John C. Calhoun, John D. Rockefeller, Teddy Roosevelt, Huey Long, Douglas Mac Arthur, and Lyndon B. Johnson. Most of the costumes were improvised, but during Halloween season, there were more available costumes for us to choose. In some cases, we went to local theater groups and rented the appropriate outfits, but that became too expensive. Unfortunately, after six years, I was the only one left to create and act out the roles as new teachers who joined the team expressed a reluctance to engage in this activity.

During the next ten years, team teaching, itself, began to fade as many of the original teachers either retired, went to the new high schools, or left education for some other pursuit. Many of the new teachers were either opposed to the concept, didn't want to role-play, or had their own agendas toward teaching subject matter. The composition of these new comers and the philosophical premises they expressed became a radical departure from the traditional methods we employed earlier. I have always felt that I learned more about education and how it should be taught during the team-teaching era then at any other time in my career.

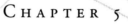

CHAPTER 5

Educational Diversity

The character of any school is really shaped by the faculty. Their strengths, weaknesses, eccentricities, and actions have the greatest influence on the environment and attitudes of the students. I cannot speak for elementary schools but this is certainly true for high schools. After the first few years of acclimating to the demands of teaching, I became more aware of my colleagues and the administrators who oversee the process. At the risk of stereotyping certain departments, I have noted certain trends and actions that tend to distinguish one group from another.

One of the reasons (perhaps the major one) I was hired was that I could coach swimming. This certainly gave me advantage over other applicants. Dealing with coaches was a lot

different than dealing with my colleagues in social studies. Most of the coaches I could get along with because I only associated with them after school. However, there was

always this feeling that I was tolerated but not welcomed in the physical education office. There was never any direct evidence of animosity but silence can sometimes speak volumes. Our head football coach was called "Tex." He was a very large, muscular person who had a Texas drawl. Where he came from in Texas, football was like a religion. He apparently graduated from a small NCAA Division II college and was probably an outstanding player. I heard from some of the other coaches that he was overlooked in the NFL draft and was embittered as a result. During my first year, he had a mediocre team and won only half of his games; however, during the next nine years he won five league championships and sustained only seven defeats. I always figured that this record would gain attention of the colleges and he would be able to go on to the next level. He had, however, certain personal proclivities that may have ultimately sealed his destiny. His extramarital affairs with wives of prominent members of the community and certain "freewheeling" female teachers gained him a great deal of notoriety. One particular episode occurred in his film room. He had a film room where he previewed and reviewed high school games. In was the only room on the campus that had this "annex." The room served more than one purpose and rumors among the faculty were rampant about what went on there. Our journalism teacher, Rudy, went to the room during one lunchtime to get some still photos of the previous Friday's game. What he encountered was "Tex" with a married teacher engaging in fornication on top of a table. The "willing partner" was furious about this intrusion and for the next four years refused to speak to Rudy. Rudy never made it public what he saw, but we managed to get the details after a few libations at the Friday "watering hole." "Tex" never said a word to him and sloughed off the whole affair as nothing significant. Unfortunately, many of "Tex's" assistant coaches were repeatedly angry about his cravings when they went away for coaching retreats and he didn't stay with them. He borrowed their cars, skipped meetings, and went out to the local bars, etc. to pursue carnal pleasures. Often times he was gone for two or three days. Apparently his wife knew of his indiscretions but didn't do anything about it.

Deke was the head basketball coach and served as chairman of the athletic department. He was always pleasant at school, but he had a drinking problem that often time got him and other coaches in trouble. He became very belligerent when he had a few drinks and most people stayed away from him because it usually led to fisticuffs. On one occasion, our athletic department hosted a league function in a nearby town where drinks were reduced to half price for the attendees. I happened to be seated with another part-time coach, Ben, who was hired as a business teacher. We were placed opposite two enormous football coaches from a rival high school who looked and acted like they could destroy both of us with one pinky finger. During the strained proceedings of the banquet, the atmosphere became tense as both "Tex" and Deke were making provocative comments to all the other coaches. Deke was "feeling no pain" when, in a drunken stupor, he got up and challenged all the coaches to come out in the nearby alley where the Starr Valley Athletic Department would "kick ass!" Ben and I immediately took off our name tags as our adversaries across the table stood up to the challenge. We both proceeded to surreptitiously head for the men's room as the room became charged with bloodlust. As we slipped out through the kitchen and headed for our cars, we heard swearing, the unmistakable sound of knuckles on flesh, and the moans of those hitting the ground. That was the last league banquet we ever attended.

Not all of our coaches fit into the characterizations above. It seemed that part-time coaches were not as obsessed with the demands and pressures that full-time coaches are faced with on a regular basis. The most vocal and active parent groups are those associated with athletics. They tend to be the most aggressive in terms of fund raising and volunteering. There seems to be a basic axiom about human behavior among the support groups that winning is everything and "woe be unto" those coaches who don't measure up. This is generally true in all aspects of American sports. As a swimming coach, I spent the first five years trying to mold a winning team with little or no support from parent groups. During the next four years the support was proportional to the amount of meets we won. In my last year, we won the league championship with a lot of support from parents who had been critical during the previous decade. I decided to bow out of coaching and turn the reins over to my assistant who, for the past three years, provided invaluable service in shaping the team. With all my best swimmers graduating, I felt it was best to get out while on top, and I never went back.

Teachers are probably the most scrutinized of any professional group in the United States. Often times they are hired to fulfill some preconceived notions expected by the community in which they serve. They are expected to do more than their job requirements and do it with a minimum of financial rewards. Each is expected to be a strict disciplinarian, an expert in their field of study, a surrogate parent, a paragon of virtue, an inspirational leader, an even-tempered adult (lacking emotional binges), and all the other qualities of adulthood that most people admire but fail to emulate. The problem with the scrutiny is that teachers are expected to rise above the human frailties and idiosyncrasies that mark the true nature of human beings, and they are judged by the community and some administrators accordingly. However, I have met very few teachers who would fulfill all the aforementioned requirements. Most of the teachers that I have known reflected some of the very best of these qualities. This was especially true during the first few years of my teaching career as I was favorably impressed with the quality of professionalism and dedication that most of them demonstrated.

During the 1970s and 1980s, the number of teachers coming into education and leaving after a short time tended to accelerate as many didn't seem to really understand what the whole education process was about. Although they didn't bring their own agendas into education, I believe that most of them who left early were either disillusioned with their roles or couldn't make it in education because of financial concerns. Most teachers who stayed in education came from a two-income family as both incomes were necessary for those who sought residences in Starr Valley during the 1970s and even up until today. Single teachers, on the other hand, had to rely upon long commutes from their homes to their jobs and many of them gave up and went into other professions.

Ned was hired in the early 1970s to teach United States History. He was an expert on colonial history and wanted to teach a whole course on that subject. Unfortunately, he never got enough enthusiasm from the students to offer a supplementary course on that period of American history. He was willing to give lectures, but not role-play, on the regular US History team which made some members rethink the whole role-playing scenario. He was fond of giving slide shows along with his lectures, but most of the slides were seventeenth-century paintings or pictures that he took while traveling back East. One particular lecture he liked to give was on colonial architecture and life styles. He gave the same lecture for two periods: one in the morning and one in the afternoon. He used a slide projector that was controlled by a remote button that he pushed during various parts of his lecture. Needless to say, most of the students were bored and very few paid any attention until on one occasion a new slide was put into the machine replacing one of the pictures. He very seldom looked at the screen while he was lecturing and seemed to have everything well coordinated. He was discussing the impact of Greek and Roman architecture on the wealthy colonial residents and how Greek and Roman statues became very popular among the gardens of the very wealthy merchants. He was discussing how the Puritans would have frowned on nude sculptures when a picture of five topless, well-developed young ladies on some beach in Europe suddenly showed up on the screen. There was a gasp from the girls in the class but no comment from any of the boys as they were probably asleep. He continued with the lecture without responding to the gasp and finished his lecture with no apparent awareness that anything was out of place. When the class was over one of the girls approached him and asked if he was aware of all the slides that he was showing. Irritated, he said, "Of course I am, I made them all myself!" The girl smiled and politely said that he should review all of them before his next lecture that was scheduled that afternoon. He didn't have much of a sense of humor and became very upset after reviewing all the slides. The problem was, who put the slide in the machine? No one claimed to have made the substitution. He was convinced that it was a student, but I was convinced in was another member of our department who was always pulling practical jokes and happened to have gone to Europe the previous Summer. When he made the correction for the afternoon class there were more students than seats and all of them were boys. They must have cut class to come in and hear his lecture.

All of them probably learned more about colonial architecture than they wanted and all left the class disappointed when the missing slide was reinstated and the substitute was removed.

Hiram was hired in the late 1970s. He entered the teaching professions late in life as he took early retirement from the bank job he had in Utah. During the first couple of years, he taught business math and statistics. His primary interest was in horticulture as he spent most of his free time planting and cultivating flowers and vegetables. After he received tenure (then it was a three-year process), the school was looking for some new class that could be a place for non-academic students who were not doing well in their regular classes. He offered to teach a class on horticulture as an alternative for the non-college bound students. Being a devoutly religious person, he was able to get his church to donate enough money to build a hot house for all his plants. The school district at that time was short on funds and gratefully accepted the generous donation. Hiram began with one period of horticulture and soon it bloomed (no pun intended) into a full time, five-period class. The class was extremely popular and of all the elective courses offered by the school, his classes filled up very quickly. However, Hiram didn't know much about botany and couldn't distinguish among many of the plant varieties. Having limited experience, he was naïve in understanding about the various forms of plants that can thrive in a hot house. One day he came into the faculty room complaining about a "weed" that was flourishing among the flowers and vegetables. He complained that for every plant that he pulled up three or four would take its place. He brought in some of the samples and we immediately recognized them as being cannabis plants. He was greatly embarrassed at not recognizing them and immediately went to the Principal who called the Drug Enforcement Agency. In a matter of hours, agents showed up at the school seeking to find out who had planted the illegal marijuana plants. Since all the students expressed ignorance of the matter, the classes were immediately shut down and all the students were assigned study hall. Hiram was then put in charge of administering five periods of study hall. The problem did not end there as some students had keys to the hot house and snuck in and continued to maintain their crop of illegal plants. Finally, the district administration sent down a maintenance crew to dismantle the hot house. The team of agents from DEA said that they confiscated over a hundred plants in the building when they did their preliminary search. The next year Hiram went back to college to get a degree in horticulture and apparently went back to Utah to teach. Hopefully, his future students in Utah were just as ignorant about marijuana as he was.

Larry and Jack were two social studies teachers who personified the very best of the qualities of professionalism and dedication. Both of them were hired a few years before I came into the fold. Both of them graduated from prestigious colleges on the west coast. They were the first group to introduce team teaching at Starr Valley High School. Both were very competent and were greatly admired by the students. Although both were married, young female students would stand in long lines at registration to get into their classes. There were many disappointed girls who missed the chance when their classes were full. As a young teacher, I looked up to both of them and appreciated their mentoring and assistance in helping me become a competent teacher. After a couple of years, Larry went into administration and became the Principal of El Norte High School after it opened in late 1960s. Jack became the debate coach and won many state awards for his dedication and achievement in statewide competitions. In the early 1970s, Jack took two of his best debaters and competed in the National Forensic Debate competition in Washington, DC. His team won second place out of over three hundred teams from throughout the United States. I learned a lot about poise, emphasis, timing, and organization from him and was able to successfully translate it into effective public speaking both in the classroom and at public meetings where I either gave a speech or served as master of ceremonies. After ten years of handling the forensics and speech classes, he went into administration and joined Larry at the new high school. Larry became one of the most popular administrators in the school district. He had an acute sense of fairness in dealing with parents, teachers, and students and had very few problems while he was Principal of El Norte High School. Both men reflected a personal magnetism that was very difficult to emulate. When I was on their United States

History team, I learned a lot about how to hold students' attention during lectures through the use of humor, anecdotal information, and properly-placed emphasis on subject matter.

Larry lost his first wife to heart disease approximately the same time I lost my first wife to cancer. We became very close and went out socializing when both of us could get babysitters. Neither one of us had any problems especially with the abundance of high school girls who were readily available and eager to help us. The only drawback to our "outings" was that most of the women we met were attracted to him and not me. But I "suffered" through the experiences and had a great time. After approximately four years of being a Principal at El Norte High School, Larry met an attractive woman who lost her husband to an automobile accident. He married her and moved to San Diego where he resumed the role of a school administrator at the district level. Five years later, he separated from his wife and moved back to Starr Valley where he resumed teaching education at a local college. After a short career teaching college, he sought a job overseas and ended up in Greece for approximately three years. Unfortunately, he came down with the most dangerous form of hepatitis after eating contaminated shellfish. With most of his liver destroyed, he came back to Starr Valley and retired until the disease finally took its toll in less than a year.

Jack decided to come back into teaching after being an administrator for five years. He got tired of all the demands placed upon him and felt that the classroom suited him more than administrative chores. We tried to resurrect team teaching but had little interest from the other teachers. We did a two-man teaching team for one year, but he suffered a stroke and wasn't able to continue in education. Unfortunately, his life was also cut short when he developed heart disease and ultimately succumbed to it a few years later.

During a eight-year span, over fifteen teachers from our district died mostly from heart disease or cancer. I knew all of them and lamented the loss of so many of my colleagues. I count my blessings that I am still alive, but I miss the companionship and camaraderie that I developed with most of them.

CHAPTER 6

The Age of Aquarius

In the latter part of the 1960s there came a new force into education. Inspired by the "Free Speech" movement, the Port Huron Statement, Vietnam protests, the Civil Rights Movement, and the "counter-culture" movement, many young people came into education and sought teaching as a vehicle for change. They were an idealistic and aggressive group who believed that through their efforts, a revolutionary new society could be created and all the traditional "evils" of American society could and would be purged. Starr Valley was not immune to the influence of this "Age of Aquarius" and many of the new teachers, especially in the social sciences and liberal arts programs, were hired to come in and effect change. The Principal of our high school was impressed with the eagerness and intentions of these newcomers and proceeded to replace many of the older retirees with this new generation. I wasn't a party to the interview and hiring process that brought many of these "new comers" to our school, but I was initially skeptical about what changes were going to take place and how they would be implemented. My skepticism was not without merit!

I met this new group, four of whom were hired to teach social studies, on the first day of school when the administration held its orientation session. Normally, this session was marked by an inspirational speech by the Principal who usually presented unrealistic goals, high expectations, and new focuses for the school year. The assistant administrators usually covered all day-to-day details of attendance procedures, grading, textbook checkouts, parking permits and the myriad of tasks and paperwork that kept the school going. Usually, all new teachers were introduced and each gave a brief, background sketch of their past experiences. On this particular orientation day, we were astounded by one of the new teachers who got up to make a prepared speech about our school and where it was heading. He was a brash, confrontational young English teacher from New York, named Lenny. He began by attacking the traditional methods of teaching and the need to change the focus and curriculum offerings for the school. He basically said that everything that was being taught was wrong and the teachers need to refocus their energies. I politely listened to what he said for the first ten minutes and then my anger took charge. Through the twenty minutes of his oration, I kept looking at the other new teachers who nodded in agreement with virtually everything he said. Finally, I had enough, stood up, and challenged him. "How can you make these assertions and assumptions when you have never been in our classrooms, seen how or what we teach?"

I received a standing ovation from the faculty as a whole. The principal had a sheepish expression marked by a deep blush and said nothing. "Tex" stood up and said to Lenny, "If you ever come in my classroom, I'll knock your teeth out!" Again, applause! The other new teachers all had frowns and glum expressions. Needless to say, the orientation came to an abrupt ending, and the optimism that usually greeted the orientation session had changed into an atmosphere of suspicion and animosity.

During the first few months of school, the climate of opinion had not changed and there seemed to be a deep division among the faculty members. This was especially true in the social studies and English departments. In the past, social studies department meetings were usually congenial, social meetings marked by frivolity and light-hearted kidding. We mostly sought consensus in making decisions, and if someone disagreed we tended to respect his or her opinions. We demonstrated respect for dissent and usually were able to get "everyone on board" with little conflict. However, a new atmosphere of tension and suspicion marked our first few meetings. The new teachers were very inflexible in trying to implement their agendas; they tended to group together and support any common views they shared. They were adamant about change and new directions rather than evaluating existing programs. The chances of cooperation and coordination on future programs seemed very remote.

Trotter was one of our new social studies teachers, and he made an indelible impression on the other department members. He was very bright and probably graduated *cum laude* from whatever college he attended. His demeanor in department meetings was one of belligerency and confrontation. He had a tendency to take issue with every point that was raised in department meetings, pointing out from his frame of reference the fallacies of our thinking and approach to teaching. Unfortunately, the other three new members tended to support everything he said. His views that history had little merit and one should never "look to the past" irked many of us who had been in education and teaching history for more than five years. He was emphatic in believing that all classes should focus on the future and not the past. I agreed with some of his premises but rejected most of the others. The problem was more than philosophical it became very polemical and unfortunately led to a permanent rift within the department. We had periodic meetings at different member's homes to "iron out" our differences but little was accomplished. The newer teachers believed that everyone needed to get high on marijuana before department business was to be conducted. The older members thought that wine and beer were more appropriate and, therefore, the generation gap widened. Soon all meetings were conducted exclusively on campus with coffee as the only liquid refreshment allowed.

Demona was the only female member of the "new breed." She had been married three times and was on her third divorce when she was hired. Her father was a controversial lawyer back east who specialized in libel and slander suits; moreover, he was one of the first lawyers to pursue sexual harassment suits and was widely quoted on nationwide television. When I was first introduced to her, I was greeted with a cold, distrustful aura that made me feel very uncomfortable. There was something in her manner that made me feel that we would never get along; therefore, I avoided her as much as I could. She never used her last name probably because she didn't know which one to use. Demona, along with all the new comers, was a firm believer in becoming pals with all her students and insisted that students refer to her as Demona rather than as Miss or Mrs. As a result of this trend many students came into classrooms and started calling teachers by their first names. The once teacher-student relationship where respect and formality once reigned had disintegrated, and it was very difficult to maintain decorum and discipline within classrooms. In spite of protests, the administration did little to curtail this development. When students came into my classroom and referred to me by my first name, I, needless to say, made it very clear where they stood in the class and what behavior was accepted and what was not; referring to me by my first name was at the top of the list. The prevailing attitude among many of the students was that the new teachers were "cool and hip" while the rest of us were remnants of the Dark Ages. Unfortunately, since all the new teachers tended to support the "pal" theory, another rift had been created. The problem wasn't exclusive to our school and was endemic through out the school district. There was always this question about where the district administration stood on this new informal and casual environment that enveloped the school and the district.

"Dr. No" was the principal. That was not his name but the label hung on him by the faculty. He earned this title, not from the James Bond novel, but by his standard response to all requests made by the faculty beyond the normal allocations. His usual response was "NO!" when additional requests were made. It took a great deal of cunning and resolve to get him to approve any financial purchase of classroom supplies beyond the regular allotment. He was not the brightest administrator and more than once would pick up on new trends and would try to implement them without understanding the full impact they would have. On one occasion, during a staff development day, he had the faculty divided into groups of fifteen. We would all sit in a circle and would have a basketball to be bounced to anyone seeking to speak to the group. No one was allowed to speak until the ball was in his or her hands. Needless to say, this did not go over very well. Another time, he divided the groups up and gave out different objects that would make noise to each group. My group was assigned glasses with spoons. I assumed the purpose was to force all the participants to stop making random noises and try to make them work together in harmony. We were told that the noise makers were designed to create a willingness to work toward group cohesion. This was even a bigger failure! Probably the worst example was the day we all were given rocks and told to sit down and write an essay on what a rock was and what impact it has on life. We were then encouraged to share our reflections and read our essays to the group as a whole. No one could figure what the purpose of all this wasted time was, and it was never made clear why we were engaging in this nonsense. Apparently, Dr. No went to some administrative retreat and was enthralled to the extent that he wanted to try it out on the faculty. Obviously, we looked forward to these time-wasting efforts with a great deal of "anticipation." I kept wondering what the taxpayers would have thought if they knew what was happening during these so-called "staff-development" days.

Staff-development days were a mixed bag of positive and negative experiences. The school district always felt that bringing outside "experts" into the schools would enrich the learning environment for the teachers. Most of these so-called "experts" had very little experience in dealing with teenagers and many of their presentations reflected this. We had an expert from Colorado who came to advocate a "school without failure" in which he believed that the best learning takes place in schools were "F" grades are nonexistent. He advocated that no one should get a failure grade in any class in high school or college. While we were listening to him, one of my colleagues stated that, "I wouldn't want to be operated on by a medical doctor who attended one of these schools!" and we all concurred. Although some of his ideas had merit, the bulk of his presentation didn't really reflect an understanding of the realities of the school environment. On one particular staff-development day, the district brought in one of the current fads that captured a lot of interest in America during the 1970s: EST training. This was the brainchild of Werner Erhard. One of his protégés led a session during one of the staff-development days at a central location for all the schools in the district. I did not attend this presentation on purpose and took a sick day. I heard a lot of conflicting views about this training. Some felt it was worthwhile while others felt it was a waste of time. One thing did occur that captured my attention. "Tex" went to the session and found out that he couldn't take a bathroom break during the presentation. His response almost brought closure to the whole day's activities. He apparently got up during the session and headed to the men's room when one of the guards told him he couldn't leave. Apparently the guard stood for a very short time in front of the exit door. "Tex" told him to "get the hell out of my way!" The guard was picked up and thrown against the wall. Another came to his rescue and he was knocked down by one punch. With both men on the floor, "Tex" said in a loud voice, "Anyone else want to stop me?" In front of the whole assemblage, he told the person in charge that this whole program was "a bunch of bull shit!" and stomped out.

The best staff-development days were the ones in which teachers from different schools within the district got together and compared notes by sharing common problems and solutions that seemed to work. Most of the shared responses could be easily adapted by most teachers if they were willing to implement them. Unfortunately, the first few of these district sessions did not work out very well. El Norte High School was the second high school founded in the valley and most of the students who attended the school came from the most affluent section of the valley. For some unexplained reason, the social studies teachers tended to have egotistical attitudes in dealing with the other high schools. During the first few district-wide staff development days they spent most of the time critiquing everyone else while adding little of their own to the proceedings. I always felt that they saw themselves as the "grand inquisitors" passing judgment upon the "peons" of the other high schools. They spent more time "dropping names" and expanding upon the conferences that they have attended or the books that they have read. Our social studies department collectively felt the same way, and we would go out of the way to ask pointed questions of their department dealing with class room issues and how each person would handle the problems of teaching subject matter. The answers we received were unsatisfactory, and when further pressed for an answer from this self-appointed "elite" group, we came to the conclusion that they had less insight into how to handle the problems than we did. Our persistence in seeking answers prompted many of them to drop the "elitist" attitudes and adopt conciliatory responses. After the first few district-wide, staff-development days, the atmosphere and willingness to work together became a reality and a lot of practical solutions to common problems became incorporated into the district-wide curriculum.

One of the most anxious moments in the career of a teacher is evaluation time. Each year teachers sweat through repeated observations followed by a formal, written evaluation. A good evaluator is worth "his or her weight in gold"; a bad one can be devastating. New teachers have the most to fear because they may be out of work with chances of ever being rehired in another district very minimal. "Dr. No" would probably tip the scale toward the bad evaluator. He was obsessed with having all the lights by the windows turned off and all windows be left open to cut down on heating or air conditioning bills. If the temperature was below 90°F., one had to turn off the air conditioning and open the windows. These two standards were always at the top of the list in the formal evaluation. The reason I would place him toward the "bad" side occurred during my tenured year. I was lecturing to a large class of over 120 students, when five minutes into my lecture he came into the room by the back door and took a seat on the last row. The door had a noticeable squeak when it opened or closed. I put in two requests to have it fixed but nothing was done. Everyone in the class became used to the noise and no one paid much attention. "Dr. No" was observing both the lights and the windows and was apparently writing down his observations when he jumped up and ran to the door. Some of the students in the back of the room looked at each other, rolled their eyes, and shook their heads while returning to take notes. Approximately twenty minutes had passed since his hasty exit when he returned with an oil can and started making squeaking noises while he lubricated the door hinges, prompting many of the students to start laughing. When he was finished, he went back to his desk, but he dropped the can and it rolled across the room with considerable noise. By then, half the class was in hysterics. I found it very difficult to look at the audience without breaking into laughter. Fortunately I was almost finished with my lecture, and I had to focus my eyes on any place but the back of the room. My evaluation regarding the lights and windows was satisfactory (the standard response), but the next point of the evaluation stated that I was "too easily distracted and maintained poor eye contact with the class!" Overall, I was given a favorable evaluation and was recommended for tenure. "Dr. No" seemed intimidated by this "new breed" of teachers and tended not to confront them on any controversial issue. Unfortunately, the new agendas put forth by this group became mired in controversy.

Gare was one of our new teachers hired to teach psychology. In a northern California county, he once ran for sheriff with no experience in law enforcement and a promise to legalize Marijuana. He was, also, an "actor" in porn films, a fact that I believe was not mentioned during his job interviews, and he showed one of them to members of the department on a social occasion,. I, fortunately, was not present at that time. Psychologically, he probably would have been a great case study for "split personalities." On some days, he would come to class with a suit, vest, and tie and would be "Mr. Straight." He would demand strict obedience and adherence to school rules and policies. No music was allowed in class, pagers were confiscated, and strict silence was demanded. Other days, he would show up in mechanic's jump suit, playing the role of "Mr. Cool." On these days, students would listen to the Rolling Stones, Janis Joplin, or Jimi Hendrix while he conducted class. I encountered him once in the men's room, standing in front of the mirror with his jumpsuit down to his ankles. He didn't have any underwear on. He asked me, "What do you think?" I beat a hasty retreat without answering him and never used that particular restroom again. The administration initially thought that these personality-switch performances were part of the class curriculum and thus did little to question his motives. However, there was a growing concern expressed by the parents as some of the young females in his class were apprehensive about his leering attitudes and overtures to them in class. On one occasion a member of the department walked in on him while he was lying on a table with his jump suit down to his waste, no undershirt and two girls giving him a back massage. He was summarily dismissed from the Psychology class but not fired. The administration was very apprehensive about this getting into the newspapers and quietly transferred him to oversee study hall while still maintaining a full salary. Instead of firing him at the end of the year, he was miraculously given a new contract and was assigned to teach English classes the following year. The older members of the faculty were astonished that he was allowed to come back and teach.

Lenny, the firebrand of the English Department, had his own problems that ultimately led to his dismissal. He instituted his own curriculum within his classes and focused on the current fads and trends with particular emphasis upon the "free love" aspects of the "flower generation." During the first month of his employment, he got rid of all the student desks and replaced them with old couches, mattresses, and thick rugs. What went on during the school day was open to speculation and none of it was favorable. On the weekends, he would have his classroom open for students wishing to engage in "homework." Most of the writing in the class was evidenced by the comments made on the mattresses. Whether Lenny was personally involved was never clear. Those who spread rumors of course came to that conclusion. Apparently, "Dr. No" came upon a weekend "homework" session when the participants were taking a break. His only comment was that, "they should keep the door closed less some one might suspect that there might be illicit activities going on!" (After all, we need to keep the campus free of controversy!) On another occasion, Lenny had all students go to a movie in a nearby metropolitan area. The movie turned out to be hardcore pornography. Most of the students said little to their teachers about the "field trip," but a few were incensed and told their parents about it. Needless to say," all hell broke loose!" Shortly before this incident the English Department wrote a collective letter to the school board demanding the Lenny either be fired or transferred immediately. When the school board met they were faced with the letter and the complaints registered by an irate group of parents. I don't know what happened in a closed session, but Lenny was gone the following day. Many of his students protested and demanded that he be reinstated. However, the permissive climate that had once existed came under tighter scrutiny and their appeal did not gain any favor.

Not all the new teachers developed questionable reputations. Chauncy was a young man who sincerely was interested in helping handicapped students and took it upon himself to create programs that would be beneficial to their learning process. He had a group of about ten students who constantly followed him around. Being single with no apparent attachments, he spent many weekends taking these students on outings. The parents believed that he was a saint, and I could hardly disagree with their assessment. Although he was hired to teach social studies classes, his efforts in helping the handicapped prompted the school district to create new and meaningful programs with him being the coordinator. After a year at Starr Valley, he became the administrator for district-wide special education programs and remained there until he was appointed to the state council for special education.

In retrospect, the "new breed" of teachers who came into the district created both positive and negative changes. It is difficult to measure and evaluate their successes and failures. On the positive side, new programs (like that listed above) were instituted with great success. The school faculty became less formal, more casual in attitudes as well as dress and, in spite of the initial confrontations, perhaps more tolerant of one another. Even Trotter, Delmona, and Gare became more flexible and lessened the intensity of their attitudes and behaviors. Gare left education soon after his efforts in teaching English proved to be disastrous. Trotter and Delmona continued to teach but only in self-contained classes and were apparently allowed to set their own standards and curriculum. I noticed that during the next two years, the more motivated and academic student stayed away from their classes and sought more traditional teachers. Delmona became one of the first teachers to transfer to the new continuation high school for students who couldn't function in regular classes. I suspect that she was very successful because she remained in this school for the next fifteen years. Trotter modified his attitudes and became interested in the fine arts where his creative instincts were appreciated. His popularity also grew and many of the artistic students took his classes. He never taught in the social studies department again.

CHAPTER 7

Teachers Unite!

In the early 1970s, there was a national, widespread unionization of teacher organizations. Starr Valley was one of the early districts in California to engage in this movement. As the district grew and new school administrations appeared, the time seemed right to promote collective bargaining and all the other advantages unionization provided. With the growing diversity of people moving into the valley, traditional animosity toward unions waned and even some parent groups openly supported this new trend. Greater salary increases and benefits enhanced the morale and attitudes of the educators who felt more like professionals. Teaching became more attractive to young people and more moderates came into the profession. Most of us who had come into the profession prior to 1965 felt comfortable and relaxed as we encountered young people who didn't have radical agendas and were more willing to listen to the "voices of experience."

Lossie (pronounced: loss-see) was part of the vanguard of the unionization movement. She had been on the staff before the influx of the "new breed" of the late sixties came on board and was eager and highly motivated to organize and lead as a teacher-representative in all labor negotiations. Personally, she was very loquacious and went out of her way to be friendly with everyone she met. At social gatherings, she tended to dominate conversations; unfortunately, discretion was not one of her strong points. Often, she would open up and relate the most intimate details of her life without considering whether her listeners were interested or not. On more than one occasion, I learned more than I wanted about her private life. Nothing, it seemed, was off limits. She was on her third husband in the early 1970s. What happened to the first two marriages, unfortunately, was brought out in graphic detail. I felt sorry for her first two husbands because I am sure they didn't want their affairs made public. I noticed that none of them remained in the area after the divorce was finalized. Her third husband was a prominent labor-relations attorney who provided immeasurable help in dealing with labor-management relations. One of her great strengths was that when she befriended you, the relationship was everlasting. She was extremely loyal and would always come to your assistance when the need arose.

Lossie tended to look at all labor-management relations in black and white terms. Labor always wore the "white hats" and management the "black hats." During most of the 1970s, relations between the district and the teachers' union were amicable and productive. We received periodic raises and our benefits packages were sound, especially because the economic well-being of California was sound and the future looked bright. Most conflicts between the administration and faculty were individual in nature. To Lossie any minor conflict between teachers and the administration was taken seriously. More often than not, she would make an issue out of a minor incident. If a teacher stubbed his or her toe on a doorjamb, she would take the initiative to represent the teacher in seeking redress of any grievances that would result. Many of the teachers felt confident and secure in the knowledge that she was there to serve their needs. I cannot help feel that the attitudes of the administration were not commensurate. With her husband an expert in the field, she would cite statutes and case studies that would reinforce her role and frustrate administrative responses.

During the 1980s, the school board became more conservative, and some of the members felt it was their duty to destroy the teachers' union. Negotiations between both groups entered into a confrontational and hostile phase. It was suspected that new school administrators were hired mainly because they were opposed to union activities. Negotiations were fraught with hostility and the unwillingness to compromise. On more than one occasion, state mediators were called in to settle the bargaining problems. Unfortunately, even their efforts led to few accomplishments. After two years with no raise, the teachers went out on a series of one-day strikes. Threats and counter-treats underscored the growing enmity between both sides. The whole affair came to the "boiling point" when the school board offered lifetime medical and dental benefits to all administrators, their wives, and personal secretaries. After two years of no raises, the union felt that this was the "last straw" and a longer strike was called. The crisis came close to physical violence as the district hired people to come in and photograph all the strikers with the intent of intimidating the younger, non-tenured teachers. The union responded with the "shadowing" technique. Volunteers among the faculty would "shadow" board members and follow them wherever they went. The Sheriff's Department was called in to harass teachers who engaged in this activity. None were arrested, but warning citations were issued. During the strikes, television stations from nearby metropolitan areas sent crews on a daily basis to cover the crisis. On another occasion, the teachers' union put up supportive signs in the faculty room encouraging all faculty members to support the actions of the union. The district administration strictly forbade any placards or signs encouraging union activities to be placed on the walls of the school. A few teachers came down after dark and moved all the signs off the wall and placed them on the ceilings. Also, some time later that night, someone broke into the faculty room and stole money from the soft drink machine, prompting the administration to call the police. No one knew who stole the money, but the police took fingerprints off the signs on the ceiling and tried to have all the teachers submit to finger printing. Some refused and the crisis deepened. No arrests were made but the growing animosity between the faculty and administration underscored the increased tensions. One teacher went so far as to rent a cement mixer for the purpose cementing the doors leading to the administrative offices. He was summarily talked out of it by "cooler heads" among the faculty. Fortunately, the whole affair came to a conclusion as a result of parent committees who sponsored a recall election for members of the school board. The teachers went back to work waiting for the results. The election became a victory for the teachers' union and the most hostile members of the board were recalled. There has never been another strike since. Lossie was in her element during this time and spent at least eighteen hours a day working on union activities as the crisis raged on. She became the president of the teachers' union and launched a new career in labor crisis management. She continued in her role as a union activist until she retired from teaching some twenty years later.

CHAPTER 8

Administrative Competence?

Augie was hired as dean of boys replacing a well-respected administrator who became principal of the new El Norte High School. I am not sure what his background was, but his actions and attitudes provoked the faculty as he embarked on a program to ensure that all discipline referrals needed to be corroborated by witnesses. This was very difficult because if a teacher disciplined an unruly student he or she had to have someone in the class (namely another student) be willing to substantiate the charge. Most of the faculty was furious about this new policy change. Faculty meetings became rancorous with venting sessions and all the enmity directed at him. He had a messianic complex as he believed that 90 percent of the referrals were unwarranted and that students had their rights being disrespected, and, therefore, he led a crusade to secure those rights. When discipline was meted out it was usually nothing more than a verbal heart-to-heart discussion. In two years, I don't believe that one student was suspended by him. Outside of heated faculty meetings, I had little contact with him until two incidents forced me to take sides. One of them occurred when I encountered a student who had not attended my class in over two weeks. I had seen him walking around campus and assumed that he had dropped the class with out filling out the necessary paper work and following the required procedures. When questioned, the student responded, "You didn't warn me that I had to be in class. Augie said that it was the teacher's responsibility to insure that all students attended class!" (this student was an eleventh grader!) I proceeded to Augie's office to discuss the matter, and his attitude was that I was at fault by failing to make it clear that attendance in my class was mandatory. For one of the few times in my career, I lost my temper and verbally assaulted him with the intention of showing how his policies were leading to disorder and chaos. The major focus of my tirade was to point out the need to inculcate responsibility among these so-called "abused children" and that wasn't being done. The student requested and got a transfer to another class.

The second incident occurred when a group of students were acting very strange around some lockers across the way from my classroom. There were about twenty or thirty of them congregating with two or three constantly looking around for any teachers. This had been going on during breaks, and especially at lunchtime. When any of the teachers ventured out into the hall, the group would quickly disperse and reform when the hall was clear. The next day the same routine was observed. Jack, the speech teacher who had a class next door, came into my class during our common prep period and said, "Have you noticed anything strange going on across the hall during breaks?" I replied that we should look into this. We both had locker keys that would open up any student lockers on campus, and we decided to do some investigation into what was attracting such a large group during non-class time. We opened up a series of lockers and found an unopened magnum of very expensive French Champagne, two half gallons of expensive bourbon, three bottles of the most expensive Italian vermouth, two large bottles of maraschino cherries and one hundred Dixie cups. We decided to pack all of them up and take them to Augie. His response was that we were violating the students' rights by utilizing unauthorized searches. He insisted that we return all the items to the lockers, and he would handle the situation. This was during the morning hours. By lunchtime, nothing had happened, and we decided to hang around outside our classrooms much to the chagrin of the students who hung around waiting for us to depart. There were quite a few irritated looks among them as we sat outside and ate our lunches. At every break, we made our presence known with friendly banter. By the end of the school day, no one came to investigate. We decided to empty the contents of the lockers and leave a note saying, "Thanks! From the phantom!" The next day, there was a lot of commotion by the lockers and a couple of students got into a fistfight. When we were breaking up the fight, I asked, "What is the problem?" The responses were all calculated to imply that it was over other issues. All the next day we kept breaking up verbal and physical tussles among the group. By the way, the liquor never found its way back into the lockers and the issue was never mentioned by either the students involved or Augie.

CHAPTER 9

Extracurricular Experiences

One of the fringe benefits of teaching high school is the Friday night football game. Seeing students in a different context is usually very rewarding. As a teacher, many students would come up to you and ask if you are enjoying the game, would introduce their friends to you and say something complementary. Usually, they would say, "he is my favorite teacher!" Whether they meant it or not, it was always a nice affirmation. The students were always excited and generally happy to see their teachers attend the games. My first football game was an event to remember. We were playing a high school that traveled a considerable distance to play our team. The name of the high school was Overfelt. Apparently it was named after some dignitary who was very influential in the community. My first reaction to hearing the name of the school was to express a relief that my daughter did not attend the school and didn't try out for any of the spirit squads. The first half of the game was boring. I believe that by half time the game was scoreless. However, the halftime festivities changed all that. A nice tradition among high schools is that during the break midway through the game the cheerleading squads would exchange sides and lead cheers for the opponent's rooting section. However, in this game our announcer made a *faux pas* that would come back to haunt him. As the spirit squads were exchanging sides, He blurted out, "Here come the Overfelt song girls!" There was a pause and then he said, "I mean here come the song girls from Overfelt High School!" The uproar and laughter from the crowd forced the girls to stop half way across the field and return to their home crowd greatly embarrassed. I am not sure why the school permitted the song girls to have the word, Overfelt, written across their bosoms with high school written around their waists but they did. That was the last time we played that school in any sport.

One of my secret desires was to some day become a sports commentator. I especially thought that broadcasting games would be fun and profitable. Being another Al Michaels, Bill Stern, or Vin Scully was something I would especially cherish. I had my chance at one of the high school football games when the regular announcer didn't show up. I was attending the game with Sam, my assistant swimming coach, when a worried administrator came up to me and asked us to fill in. Both Sam and I went up to the booth and thus began my short-lived "dream come true." We decided that instead of relating the game in the past tense: "the ball was carried by Joe Smith for five yards!" we would liven up the game by doing a play by play with Sam filling in as the color analyst. We were having a great time until one of the assistant coaches came up during the game to tell us that "Tex" was getting mad because we were informing the opposing team about the plays before they began. It was all speculation, but unfortunately, most of what I anticipated was going to happen did occur. We won the game by over fifty points, but that didn't placate "Tex." The next home game we tried to tone down any predictions about what the play was going to be and narrated the action instead. We continued to broadcast most of the games during that year. However, our commentary came to end when during a half-time performance we inadvertently left the microphone on. Cookie was one of the flag girls who was notorious for tripping over anything in her way. Both Sam and I had her in our classes and could attest to her clumsiness. She was a really nice girl and fairly good student, but kids would laugh at her when she constantly stumbled over objects such as rugs, bags, or books on the floor. I believe that her parents encouraged her to become a flag girl hoping that she would overcome her problems. It must have been very difficult for her to perform in front of a large crowd, but I will give her credit that during her routines she would remain upright. During the last game that we did any announcing, we forgot to turn off the mike during halftime. When Cookie and her retinue had finished their routine and were heading off the field, Sam bet me a beer that she would trip over the tarpaulin that was behind the players' bench. I should have suspected something when the crowd grew unexpectedly quiet. As predicted, she tripped over the tarp and fell flat on her face. The crowd let out with a roar and yelled out, "How about a beer for us?" After many apologies and a letter to the parents, we were never invited to announce games again. Cookie, however, was very gracious in her attitude toward us. Later on, she said that she heard our comments and decided to trip for the fun of it. Whether it was true or she was trying to placate us remains unclear.

High school extracurricular activities often times provided teachers opportunities to make some extra money. Teachers were hired to sell tickets, patrol parking lots, and help administrators do their jobs especially at highly-attended athletic contests. After football games, there were postgame dances. Chaperones were necessary, and they were initially paid by the school. After about three years, the school decided it was becoming too costly and planned on canceling all postgame activities. I volunteered to continue the dances through the auspices of the recreation department by convincing the administration that the dances could become self-supporting by charging the students more money for attendance. The school administrators were leery of any new programs, especially where students were charged more money, but they went along with the idea on a trial basis. Sam and his wife became willing partners and we embarked on self-supporting program designed to give students a place to go after games. Our efforts were very successful. We even had enough money to hire local bands to come in and play. When the school ran the dances, a disc jockey was hired to play tapes and records. Now it was possible to hire live bands and make money over and above the costs. We hired teachers to come in and help chaperone, and as attendance grew, the whole project became a financial success. In spite of the volume of the noise, the dances were always crowded and all the students seemed to have a great time.

However, some of the bands we hired were not very good. On one occasion, we hired a group of students from the high school to perform. When the time came to perform, the whole band froze up and wouldn't play. The students were getting restless and started calling band members names. Sam stepped in and told the band that if they didn't start playing that he would grab the microphone and start singing. The band quickly forgot their stage fright and began performing. The biggest problem with the performances was the noise level. While we were running the dances, we used earplugs to drown out the noise, but even that was not sufficient. After a year of hiring very poor local bands, the students decided to try to get better quality bands from outside the area and were willing to pay more money to get better quality. I, personally, never liked rock music, but the quality of the performances during the ensuing years was a remarkable improvement over the local teenage bands.

The biggest problem we had at the dances was the conduct of the football players. Of all the athletes in the school, football players were the most difficult to deal with. They tended to strut around campus acting like little "gods." Of course this behavior was encouraged by their adoring fans, especially impressionable young girls. Very few football players ever made an effort to buy dance tickets and relied on either having girls pay their way or try to sneak them into the dances. The dances were held in an old combination multipurpose room and girl's gym built by the PWA during the Depression. It had more windows, doors, and access points than any other building on the campus. Typically, girls would pay their way into the dance and retire to the girls' locker room where windows and doors were opened to their "heroes." As the problem grew, the need for more female chaperones did as well. In spite of having to pay more wages to the increased numbers of chaperones, we continued to make money. Some of the chaperones were worthless especially when problems ensued. On one occasion, we were busy checking kids into the dance, when a male chaperone came running up to Sam and me, proclaiming that somebody was trying to break down the door in the back of the room. Both of us left our posts and ran to the back of the building. We opened the door expecting a group of football players, but what we encountered was a young ninth grader who weighed all ninety pounds knocking at the door. When questioned, he said that he went out to get some fresh air and inadvertently closed the door behind him. The chaperone was suitably embarrassed and never volunteered again.

Besides the on-going problem with the football players, the parking lot in front of the building became a perpetual headache. We hired private security guards to patrol the area but little was accomplished as most kids in cars paid little attention to the "rent-a-cops." We were advised to contact an organization located in one of the surrounding metropolitan areas. For the next month, we had hired the best and scariest security guards to ever come to Starr Valley. On the first night, three very muscular Afro-Americans showed up. All three sported Afro hairstyles, had tight-fitting uniforms accentuating their muscles, and wore dark glasses. (This was nighttime!) When I met the leader, I was a bit apprehensive. All three were very polite and took their tasks seriously. I assigned them the duties of moving people out of the parking lot, checking the periphery for anyone attempting to sneak in, and keeping a watch out for potential problems. When I went out to check them out, the parking lot was free of loiterers, there were no football players attempting their Friday night rituals, and the whole area was quiet and peaceful. I continued to hire this agency until the district administration called me in to answer the charges that I hired a bunch of thugs who threatened the students. I contacted a group of students who encountered the security guards and not one of them complained about their actions. The consensus of opinion was that they were scary but firm and polite in dealing with any problems. Unfortunately, I was given the mandate to not hire this group again. It didn't take very long before the problems resumed.

One of the down sides of chaperoning extracurricular events was the problem of drinking. We had to be constantly vigilant in dealing with students who imbibed prior to an event. It was extremely difficult to curtail the "partying" that took place. If we suspected a student of being drunk, our first order of business was to separate him or her from friends and call the parents to come pick up the student. This took a lot of time and effort forcing us to neglect our other responsibilities. To turn away students who were drunk was to invite disaster. Friday night dances tended to have the most problems. Our general rule was to allow students who came to the dance right after the game to be admitted with out question. It was the students who came to the dance after about fifteen or more minutes after the game who were carefully monitored. We were forced to close the doors and not allow admission after fifteen minutes, but we still had problems with those who tried to sneak into the dance through the other access points. On one occasion, one of the janitors who was working the night shift at school came over and said that there was a serious problem on campus. Apparently a young ninth-grade girl was "entertaining" a line of boys in one of the school wings. When the janitor came upon the scene, all the boys except one took off running. They were having sex when the janitor yelled at them. He said that, "the girl told him to (expletive) off! He wasn't finished!" By the time Sam and I appeared on the scene, everyone was gone. We found an empty six pack of beer in the bushes. Afterwards, the school put up fences and locked all the hallways, but the amount of "partying" continued to plague most school functions. With the exception of the aforementioned problems, the dances were efficiently run and all profits gained as a result were turned over to student government. We continued to host postgame dances for approximately nine years. In the early 1980s, the Student Council decided that they wanted to run the dances and we bowed out. Unfortunately, they were unwilling to pay teachers to chaperone the dances and had volunteer parents take their place. The dances became beset with a myriad of problems forcing the administration to shut them down.

CHAPTER 10

Driver Training and Other Horrors

One of the best ways to get extra money in education was to become a driver-training instructor. I learned this during my first year of teaching. At that time, all one needed was a General Secondary Teaching Credential to get behind the wheel with a group of two or three students. We mostly taught it after school, on Saturdays, or during vacations, and the money came in handy when our salaries weren't enough to compensate for unexpected bills, entertainment expenses, and vacations. The work was similar to what I suspect happens to soldiers during combat where there are hours of boredom punctuated with minutes of sheer terror. One of the best comedy routines I have ever seen was Bob Newhart's rendition of the "driver training instructor." I laugh every time I hear or see it performed on television. It was easy to identify with the character portrayed.

Most of the students we had were fairly proficient in their driving skills with approximately one out twenty never having any experience. These few, however, were the challenges that made us earn our money. As Starr Valley grew with more and more subdivisions being built, the number of streets and areas to teach behind-the-wheel training made our tasks a lot easier. The problem was freeway and highway driving. For the most part, we had to take the students approximately ten miles away to get any practice. We usually saved this part of instruction until last or a least until students demonstrated enough proficiency to do it earlier. I had one experience that came close to being my last one. I had a girl student who very nervous and sometimes erratic in her driving habits. I thought that on the second to the last day I would give her a chance to drive on a major highway when traffic was the lightest. Approximately eight to ten miles from Starr Valley there was an interstate highway where the speed limit was sixty-five miles an hour. The highway had "turnabouts" where drivers going east could take one of them cross into oncoming traffic and proceed west. In any case, one had to stop for oncoming traffic before proceeding to make the turn. We had gone approximately two miles when I told her to take the next turn, stop and proceed when it was clear. I noticed that a four-axle truck was approaching at a high rate of speed in the near or fast lane. She hit the brake and then, for some unexplained reason, the gas pedal. We shot across two lanes of traffic into a ditch where I wrestled control of the car away from her. The truck blew its horn and swerved to miss us by taking out three or four signs before coming to a complete stop a hundred yards down the road. If any car was in the slow lane, I wouldn't be writing this memoir. The girl became hysterical and started crying. The other two girls in the car started screaming. I had to drive the girls back to school, but not before I checked out the truck driver. His hands were glued to steering wheel and his eyes were bulging out of his head. We checked the truck and there was very little damage. I told him that I would call the California Highway Patrol from the next exit, but he was reluctant to make out any reports and muttered something about his driving record. With three near hysterical and crying girls, I left the scene and took them home. As we were leaving, the truck took off very quickly and proceeded along its way. That night was what I call a "three-martini night!" The student driver, needless to say, did not pass driver training; in fact, she flunked it seven times afterward. I never did find out whether she ever did get her license.

Some experiences can be very embarrassing. On one occasion, a woman was driving an expensive fiberglass sports car behind our vehicle. We were approaching a freeway from an onramp and our car had to stop for the oncoming traffic. I happened to notice in the rear view mirror that the sports car was not slowing down and the driver was looking

over her shoulder. I yelled to the kids in the car to brace themselves as she suddenly hit the brakes and spun into the rear of the driver training car. I immediately checked to see if everyone in the car was all right. Nobody complained, so I got out of the car and the woman was furious as the whole front end of her fiber glass car was "totaled." As the woman stormed out of her car, she failed to recognize the California highway patrol officer who was tailing her up the onramp. I am sure that she was immediately going to blame us for the accident, but when she saw him, she sat down and cried. While we were filling out the reports, the woman informed us that she had just picked up the sports car from the dealer and was going to surprise her husband at work. The officer started tailing her when she was exceeding the speed limit before entering the onramp. The only damage to the driver training car was a slight dent on the bumper guard. There were no injuries to anyone involved.

Another incident was, perhaps, more embarrassing. In the hills to the west of Starr Valley, there was a very steep hill where the road was recently paved and curbs were put in. The developer was planning multiple residences in the million-dollar range. The hill was a popular rendezvous spot for nighttime activities involving teenagers. It was also a excellent place to teach hill driving and parking. One Saturday, I was training three students in the proper and legal form for hill parking. At the top of the hill, there was a cul-de-sac where it was possible to turn the car around without having to stop and use reverse. There was a SUV parked there with apparently no one in it. Our student kept getting closer to the vehicle and I told him to turn the wheel more to avoid contact. He, unfortunately, nudged the SUV and two heads popped up from the back seat. Both of them were nude from the waist up and the girl screamed, "My God, It is Wildes!" and dove under the blanket. Both of them were my students in American Government. The boy put on his pants and stepped out of the car to inspect the damage. There wasn't any major damage but a slight scratch on the bumper. He demonstrated no signs of embarrassment and kept his shirt off while we were discussing the incident. The girl never got out from under the blanket. Since there was negligible damage and by mutual consent no reports were filed, and the boy went back into the vehicle. Five minutes later, they passed our car, and we all waved at them. For the next two months, the girl would not look at me and would come into class with her head down and a very obvious blush on her face. I always greeted her as though nothing had happened and never brought up the incident. I always had the impression that the boy wanted the whole school to know about what a "stud" he was and was wishing I would bring out the incident in class. I never gave him that satisfaction and ignored all references to it.

I could never know what kind of student took driver training. One student was driving along a crowded street in one of the nearby towns when I noticed that she was driving with her head cocked to one side and kept getting close to other vehicles. I kept warning her to be careful as she was almost side-swiping cars to the left of the driver training vehicle. Finally, I had to grab the wheel out of her hands and pull the car over. When I asked her, "Can't you see how close you are to the vehicle on the left?" She responded, "I am sorry but my left eye is made of glass!" I am not sure under what circumstances the State of California would grant drivers licenses to one-eyed persons, but I had to flunk her. On another occasion, I had a young girl who was improperly dressed and arrived on a Saturday smelling like a distillery. She was left off by some disreputable-looking adult who departed very quickly. Since it was Saturday and the school was closed, we drove her home and her parents were not there. A couple of the girls who were also training that day took her into the house and we left. Approximately two hours later, a California highway patrolman pulled us over and said that the parents had called the police accusing me of kidnapping the girl. Apparently she made a date with some adult and told her parents that she was going to driver training at 8:00 AM. The actual class didn't start until 1:00

PM. It took a while and a few phone calls to straighten out the problem. The girl apparently went into a guest bathroom and fell asleep in the bathtub. Why the parents called the police and accused me of kidnapping her was never quite clear. I never did get an apology from the parents. The California Highway Patrolman was very polite and recognized that the whole affair was a big mistake.

After teaching driver training for approximately five years, the State of California came down with a directive that all instructors had to have a specialized credential to continue teaching. All the teachers in the State were required to take the appropriate classes to fulfill the necessary requirements. Approximately ten of the instructors who taught in both of the high schools in the district signed up for this one class taught by a person with a Doctorate in Driver Education degree. He did his research on comparing female driver training instructors (there were only five in the whole State) with their male counterparts. I am not sure what school would offer such a degree, but we, who had endured these sessions, came to the conclusion that it must have been *S*am *H*ouston *I*nstitute of *T*echnology, or more appropriately the acronym, because of the value and worth of what was taught. For example, on one session, he spent forty-five minutes explaining twelve ways to take roll in a driver training car with four pupils. His exams were old Vehicle Code Exams put out by the Department of Motor Vehicles with an added section of true/ false questions. Every question in this section was considered by experienced teachers to be invalid because of the way it was written. He would never admit that his exams had little value in qualifying instructors toward the new credential.

Sam and I volunteered to teach a nine-week class on driver education, the classroom requirement for getting a license. We were assigned the cafeteria to team-teach 115 students during the last period of the school day. The cafeteria had no desks, and we were forced to teach the class utilizing luncheon tables where half the class faced us and the other half had their backs to us. Needless to say, the conditions bordered on the impossible. The students who had their backs to us were making faces and other disruptive gestures to those who were facing us. Discipline was very difficult to maintain. We tried lecturing, but that was almost impossible. We decided to line up a group of guest speakers from insurance companies, the Highway Patrol, auto mechanics and anyone who could capture the interest of the class. The most student attention was given to the movies: "Red Asphalt" and "Code Three" which were supplied by the Highway Patrol. I believe that we showed both features at least three times during the session. To keep the students focused we broke up the class into small groups and stationed them at various points in Starr Valley observing driver behavior. Each person was given a check list of observable driver infractions. We did this at least twice a week and tallied all the results by the end of the nine-week period. Examinations were out of the question because of the close proximity of the students to each other. We decided to have the students give individual oral reports or short group-research assignments. After the nine-week session was over, we never volunteered again to teach the class room phase. I felt sorry for the teachers who were assigned to teach the class from that point on.

Educational Pedagogy

In the last ten years of my career, I was approached by many of the young teachers asking my opinion on a number of teaching techniques, especially those that were successful. I was always cautious about how to approach the subject without being too dogmatic or didactic in relating my own philosophy of teaching. I was always happy to help them when they were having problems, but I never went out and forced my opinions on any of them. One of the personal observations I made about teachers is that each is very protective and even covetous about their classroom and methods of teaching. To avoid any potential conflict or animosity, I believe that it is important to recognize that fact and accept it. I always prefaced any advice I gave by stating that what works or worked for me doesn't necessarily mean that it will work for everyone. Furthermore, any advice I give should be modified to suit the needs of the teacher. Once this was made clear, an open and worthwhile dialog could begin. Many of the problems are endemic in education. Some examples are how does one establish discipline? How does one check on homework to see if it was shared with other students? What kind of tests are the most effective? How does one minimize cheating on tests? How does one minimize plagiarism in research assignments? How does one encourage discussion in classes? And, most significantly, how does one get students to take charge of their own learning? In the following paragraphs, I will try to address each one without being too pedagogical.

Discipline in the classroom is one of the overriding problems faced by teachers in all schools and especially in high schools. Methods of dealing with this problem vary according to circumstance. In the inter-city schools, I assume the problems are different than in middle-class suburban schools and the criteria for dealing with each must take into account those differences. I cannot speak for how to handle a problem in an inter-city high school because I have never taught there. Starr Valley High School was, and is, an upper-middle class school with approximately 95 percent of the students going on to another level of schooling once they have graduated. As a male teacher who is over six feet, two inches and weighing approximately 225 pounds, I have had fewer discipline problems than a five-feet-two-inch female weighing 110 pounds. Women teachers face more challenging discipline problems than their male counterparts. One of the first pieces of advice I received from one of the social studies teachers who helped me during my first year was to never smile in class until December then only if the students are respectful and afraid of your authority. I found that very difficult to do and couldn't maintain that image. Another piece of advice from the same teacher was to pick on the quietest and nicest girl in class and verbally reprimand her for any minor infraction in a loud and stern voice in front of the class; the point being, that any unruly student who would normally "act up" would be leery of trying to "test the teacher" if that is the way the teacher would respond to a minor infraction by one of the better students. Again, I never tried this approach. What, then, did I do to establish discipline? First of all, I never allowed high school students to choose their seats, and I assigned them seats on the first day of school. To wait any longer was to suggest a weakness that could be exploited by those students who spend an inordinate amount of time during the first few days trying to "size you up." Secondly, one should spell out the rules of conduct without overemphasizing the punishment aspect. To focus too much on the disciplinary aspects of wrong classroom behavior usually is an indicator that one had problems in the past and couldn't handle them thus inviting someone to test him or her again. Thirdly, one should always have some work for them to do in class. At the beginning of the year, one has to assume that students are primed and ready to do work. If I had a disciplinary problem, I had the student stay behind in class where I firmly: "laid down the law." I believe that reprimanding a student in front of the whole class was counterproductive and usually resulted in promoting sympathy for the perpetrator. If a student doesn't respond to my warning about staying after class, I would ask the student to leave the class and go down to the dean's office or to his or her counselor. In all cases, I believe that it was of paramount importance to never lose one's temper in class. One of the most effective ways of dealing with an unruly student after class is to look him or her in the eyes and in a very firm, but not loud, tone of voice, say, "If you are not old enough to understand the rules of this class, it might be better to go to your counselor and ask for a class where the rules are simplified and you can handle them!" This usually works! The major axiom dealing with student behavior is to use psychology in establishing and maintaining discipline.

Homework is one of the ongoing problems of teaching. The question of how much or little one requires is up to the individual teacher. I have always believed that each teacher should make up all the assignments for the first semester or least the first nine weeks before the school year begins. I tried to give a semester worth of homework on the first day of class with the stipulation that each assignment will be due on certain calendar days. I do not believe that assignment be given on one day and make it due the next day. I always had a weekly chart on the board with homework assignment due dates on it. One of the ways to encourage passive learning is give an assignment and make it due the next day. If the student knows on Monday that the homework is due, say Thursday, he or she can plan ahead to do the assignment. This is preferable to having students wait until told what to do and then react (passive learning). Most students do not budget their time and plan ahead. If the assignment is not complete by the due date, the teacher can dismiss the usual complaint that, "I didn't have time!" For those students going to college, the twin problems of budgeting time and planning ahead are two of the main obstacles they have to overcome. Unless they learn how to do both in high school, they will have a major problem coping with the demands of college work.

One of the endemic problems of homework assignments is the inevitable sharing of answers among students. Teachers have to recognize this fact and adjust their requirements to account for this inevitability. To spend time trying to figure out who did what to get the answers is too time-consuming and frustrating. There are a few tricks that I have found to have worked in dealing with this problem. Remember, that once the students leave class, maintaining control over where they get the answers to the questions becomes almost impossible. I find this to be true that even among the best students in the class where the sharing of answers on homework assignments is commonplace. There are ways of dealing with this issue. One is to check to be sure that all parts of the assignment are both complete and thorough by focusing in on one part of the assignment for careful analysis and commentary while superficially scanning the rest of the assignment. When students come to class on due dates, the teacher should arbitrarily assign students to write and explain their answers on the board. If a student copied someone else's work, he or she would have a difficult and the embarrassing task of trying to explain the answers. Another, less desirable, way to deal with identically-worded homework is to give a good grade to one and a poor grade to the other. Inevitably the student with the poor grade will come up to complain and demand that he or she get the same grade as the other student. In this case, the teacher would read both and say, "You are right! I am glad you pointed out this discrepancy!" Then the better grade should be lowered to the poor grade. This method should be used only after a series of warnings about copying assignments have been made, and the students continue to pursue the same course of action. Probably, the best way to minimize sharing of answers is to collect the homework at the beginning of the class and hand out paper with the intention of having the students answer one part of the assignment as a quiz without using their notes. Students who copy someone else's work very seldom spend the time to read what was written and therefore will not do well. To maintain academic integrity, I feel that it is important not to count homework as much as exams, or one should emphasize in-class work where the opportunity to copy is minimized.

What type of exams are the best? The best measure of how much a student has learned in the social sciences is to require essay exams. The best type of essay exam is one in which there is a definite answer and does not allow the student to generalize or offer opinions on the subject matter without substantial evidence used in support of the thesis statement. For example, a question in American history that states, "Define the concept of Social Darwinism and explain how and why the ideas expressed were used to justify the accumulation economic power and wealth among the 'Captains of Industry' during the latter part of the nineteenth century!" is preferable to one that states," What was the impact of Social Darwinism on American history during the post–Civil War era?" The first question asks the student to examine the basic ideas held by the Social Darwinists and how big businessmen used these ideas to justify their actions. The second question is too broad and can lead to a multitude of views where opinions are expressed but proper focus is not apparent. In grading the second question, the teacher is facing a series of pitfalls and will have difficulty in explaining why students received the grades earned. The biggest problems with essay exams is the amount of time spent grading each paper and making the appropriate comments. I believe that the primary responsibility of grading this type of exam must rest with the teacher and not with other evaluators, such as teacher or student aides. When teachers have classes in excess of 125 students a day, full essay exams are time-consuming to grade. Unless students have demonstrated proficiency in writing skills, such as in advanced placement or honors classes, regular students should be given short-answer questions that can be easily graded and the answers reflect understanding of what was emphatically brought out in class. Such questions as, "Develop in three paragraphs, with specific reference to programs or actions, the major complaints leveled at the New Deal by the conservatives of the Republican Party during the 1930s!" are preferable in regular classes to, "Evaluate the criticisms leveled against the New Deal by the Liberty League during the 1930s!" The second question is more appropriate for Advanced Placement and Honors classes because it allows the student to expand on a fundamental understanding of both philosophies and apply it to the evaluation. The former question, although simplistic, tests the student's understanding and development of both the significant programs and the conservative reactions.

Multiple-choice exams are a good alternative and easy to grade, but whether the answer was a product of guess work or acquired knowledge is hard to determine. This type of exam should be given only as an adjunct to the essay. If a teacher is under the stress of getting grades completed in a short time, it is a good substitute and a less fretful way of accomplishing the task. The major problem of multiple-choice tests is getting the right question aligned with the subject matter or skills that need to be measured. In the forty plus years that I have been teaching, I have found very few questions that fit that criterion, unless I make them up myself. Standard multiple-choice questions that are published along with the textbook tend to be exercises in "trivial pursuit" and usually have little validity in the proper measurement of learning. The other major problem of multiple-choice exams is trying to minimize cheating. In order to accomplish this, the teacher needs to have at least two or preferably three different versions of the same test. Again, this is a very time-consuming effort, especially if he or she is making up the questions. On more than one occasion, I have had students turn in answers for the wrong version of the test. Some time ago, I had a very bright young man who took a multiple-choice test and got a 100 percent. In the next aisle, two young girls missed 100 percent on the test. When I turned back the exam I didn't explain that there was more than one version until we had critiqued the exam. Both girls protested that, "I was unfair!" until I explained the multiple-version scenario. The silence in the classroom was deafening.

The worst type of exam is the true/false type of test. There is virtually no validity in measuring learning through this type of test.

When I was taking the driver-training course and the instructor made half the exam into true/false questions, there was a virtual rebellion among my classmates who protested the wording of the questions, which inevitably led to arguments. The instructor was unwilling to accept criticism until we threatened him with a collective letter signed by all to the State Department of Credentials. But by the time we were planning to send the letter, the class was over and we all passed. For our purposes, the matter became moot, and no further action was taken by us.

One of the major problems educators are facing today is the growing influx of plagiarism in research papers. The problem is evident in colleges, high schools and even in elementary schools. The difficulty for teachers is proving that the written work was a product of plagiarism, and without evidence, the task becomes very difficult. The internet has facilitated the process of obtaining written papers for a fee. Unless the teacher carefully monitors the process of research, the odds are that any finished paper will have been plagiarized. It is almost impossible to completely eliminate plagiarism in research. There are, however, a few techniques that can facilitate the process and lessen the chances.

First, if a student if given the opportunity to choose the topic, the teacher must insist that the student define the parameters of the research by limiting the topic, placing it within a definite time frame, and narrowing the focus. The student should seek as many sources dealing with the topic as possible. I made it a requirement of at least twenty-five with no reference to internet sources. If the student could not find twenty-five sources, he or she would have to change the topic, time frame, focus, or choose a new subject. Within a short time period, the students need to submit a list of the sources with attention given to proper bibliographic form. In history classes, the teacher should be able to look at the bibliographical entries to determine which of the sources could be valuable and which are questionable and indicate those to the student before research is started. Once research is started, the teacher needs to monitor the note taking and periodically check on each student's work. I believe that all research notes need to be turned in before an outline of the paper is submitted. The teacher needs to peruse the notes with the topic, focus, etc. in mind. One of the problems of reviewing student-research notes is what they write. Most tend to take random notes that upon reading give little or no direction in determining the focus of the topic. I believe that it is of paramount importance to keep the students on task and monitoring this phase of research is critical. The research phase, obviously, will take the longest time and daily excursions to the school or local libraries should be a top priority. After the research phase, an outline with a well-defined thesis statement is in order. This should be submitted at least one week before the final paper is due. I believe that the teacher has an obligation to spell out the rubric for grading the paper before the final paper is submitted. I, also, believe that the above steps need to be proportionally figured into the final grade of the paper.

Secondly, I would prefer to provide a list of questions from old Advanced Placement or SAT II essay exams and have the students choose one of them to do research on. I would utilize the same processes as above and would monitor their research in the same way.

In my Advanced Placement United States History classes, I required the students to read a chapter out of Alexis De Tocqueville's, *Democracy in America*, entitled, "Tyranny of the Majority." From discussion and common agreement, the students could develop certain criteria whereby a "tyranny" could be determined. Each student would then use the criteria as a basis for doing research on another period of American history where it was assumed that a "tyranny" existed. The most common topics were the Indian removal programs during the Jacksonian era, the relocation of Japanese-Americans during World War II, or the plight of minorities in seeking equal rights in American history. Using the processes previously discussed, the students proceeded to do their research. Being an

Advanced placement class, the demands and requirements were more rigid, but the results can be well worth the effort. I also kept the finished papers so that I wouldn't be getting the same paper from future students. This, of course, requires that you have proper storage facilities for the papers.

In the last two examples of types of research papers, I found that the problem of plagiarism could be minimized as the focus of each type of paper was more specific and irrelevant material could be easily ferreted out. In dealing with the "Tyranny" paper, it was easier to grade because most of the requirements required critical thinking especially as it applied to proof. Students were less inclined to jump to conclusions and more likely to look at their research as plausible hypotheses.

When I was teaching regular (not honors or advanced placement) United States History, I required that all students seeking and A or B in the class do a research paper. As above, I tried to limit the topics and tried to make the paper short in length with a lot of emphasis upon what the student thought about the subject. Plagiarism was a major problem, and unless I took the previously mentioned steps, it was almost guaranteed. I collected the papers first and handed out paper to each student to write out in his or her own handwriting the major points that were covered in the research paper. I usually read this first before I read the original paper. On one particular occasion, I gave a student a low grade and received a phone call from his mother demanding that we have a conference with a counselor and an administrator present. At the conference, I pointed out that the student didn't know anything about what was written in the paper. Secondly, I pointed out some serious omissions and faults in the original paper. The mother told me that she graduated *cum laude* from Cornell University and thought the paper was excellent. The more I took the time to point out the failures in the original paper the madder she became. She said that she knew a History professor who would review the document, and then she would take appropriate legal action against me. When she left, we all came to the conclusion that the woman wrote the paper and her son didn't read what she wrote. Some time later the administrator received a letter from the History professor exonerating my grading techniques and praising the manner in which research at the high school level was being conducted. He added that he would have given the same grade if one of his students turned in that paper in his college class.

Another problem in teaching students in Social Studies classes is promoting discussion. Most high school students are reluctant to discuss any of the issues raised in class. I believe that the reasons for this reluctance are based upon certain fears: one, they don't want to offer an opinion out of fear of being wrong; second, many of them don't want to speak out because of the perceptions and judgments of their peers. In Advanced Placement and Honors classes, the problem of discussion among the students is less than in a regular class. In the advanced classes, the students recognize their own intellectual capabilities and are willing to debate issues and engage in meaningful dialogue. In regular classes, there is a great reluctance to engage in intellectual discussion. I believe that many of the students in these classes are fearful of being labeled as "egg heads" or worse among their peers.

To encourage discussion among regular students, I have found some techniques that have worked. One, I believe that every student should be told at the beginning of the year that discussion is an integral part of the total grade in the course. Second, I gave point credit to any student who would come up with "probing questions." Questions that begin with "how" or "why" should be rewarded with some type of credit given. I always prefaced this credit by stating that the question is open for discussion; if it can't be answered by me or the textbook it becomes the basis sharing of opinions without the threat of being graded down. I encourage students to question motives by historical figures under study.

Even if I know the answer to the question, it is imperative to draw out answers from the students and encourage debate among them before bringing on closure. One of the most effective motivators in encouraging discussion is the evaluation process. For example, I have had students grade Presidents by assigning grades A through F in judging their actions on controversial issues. The most controversial Presidents are the easiest to judge. One of the evaluation subjects was Franklin D. Roosevelt. After an in-depth study of FDR and the New Deal, I had the students give him grades on the most controversial actions he took during the Great Depression. Among his actions, I had the students grade him on the use of Keynesian Economics, the establishment of the Tennessee Valley Authority, and his "court-packing plan." When the students had given him a grade for each action, I tallied the results and asked them to justify the grades. The students who gave him the most extreme grades were asked to explain why they believed he deserved those grades. It was extremely important to not criticize the students on their choices. The only thing I did was to ask questions in order to clarify their positions. I have never, in all the years of teaching United States History, failed to provoke discussion through this process. The biggest problem was not completing all the evaluations before the end of class. Another way to provoke discussion is play the "devil's advocate" by taking and defending an unpopular view. This is probably the most commonly used technique in high school classes. One has to be very careful in exercising this technique. I have played this role on numerous occasions and had negative "feed back" from parents who didn't understand the purposes behind taking these positions.

The most significant advice I can give teachers deals with the problem of students taking the initiative in their learning. This is the prime objective of all evaluations of public education, as it should be! This is probably the most difficult task educators face in the public school system. I cannot speak for science, math, physical education or any other departments in public schools, and the advice I present has only applied to social studies classes and only to students who have the intelligence but for whatever reason are not exercising it. Unfortunately, this seems to be the majority of students in those classes. The first rule in motivating students is to build self-confidence. At the beginning of the school year, I give "open note" exams to all regular (not honors or advanced) classes. I usually begin with a combination multiple choice and fill-in type of exam, which covers all the material up to the point of the exam. After grading the exam, I make the students review all their wrong answers by looking at their notes. They are required to do a critique of their responses by searching their notes for the correct answers. If they find the answers and have enough information to correctly answer the questions, they are then required to add the "corrected score" to their original grade to see what they should have received. The students are then required to turn in the critique with all their notes and the answers highlighted. If the students couldn't find the answers in their notes, they should know why they weren't there. If students shared homework answers with others and the notes received were insufficient or nonexistent, they can hopefully remedy the situation. The second exam of the year and all subsequent exams were closed note: meaning they would have to study. I utilized this process through the first semester of class especially for students who fared poorly on the exams. Self-confidence stems from the opportunity of the student to evaluate his or her own work. It becomes a diagnostic tool to promote initiative and self-direction. Not all students learn or become motivated as a result of this process, but I have found that the majority of regular or average students that I have had tend to be more responsive and get better grades as a result. With regard to how to apply this process to educationally-handicapped students, I would have to leave that to experienced teachers who work with them.

I have found that one of the most effective ways to build self-confidence is to offer "creative projects." I usually will present the students with a historical concept and have them do a presentation in a novel or different way. Many of the resultant projects were worth the effort put into them by the students. I have received editorial cartoons, scripted short plays, role-playing performances, homemade videos, and a variety of audio/visual presentations. On one remarkable occasion, I had a group of boys who were all doing poorly on regular class room requirements. I told them that they should choose a current, hot political issue and use a camcorder to do some interviews outside of school. They chose the issue of animal experiments to advance scientific knowledge. They chose three locations to do their interviewing. First, was an upscale shopping center where expensive boutiques, clothing stores, and restaurants catered to a very wealthy clientele. They interviewed approximately ten people and the responses were relatively the same: "animals, except pets, have no rights and must be used for scientific experimentation in order to better the lives of humans!" Their interviews were cut short when one of the "divas" complained to the security personnel that she was being harassed. The whole episode was captured on tape and from all indications the four did not argue or in any way make derogatory comments to the woman. They were, however, asked to leave and warned that they could not conduct interviews without a permit. Second, they went to a rock concert and interviewed approximately thirty people. Some of them were high on drugs, which the interviewers pointed out during the shooting session. The most coherent answers followed a predictable pattern as most of the people who responded stated, "animals have rights just like humans, and not enough is being done to protect or preserve these rights!" The third location was in downtown Starr Valley where a greater variety of people were interviewed. In this session, approximately thirty people were interviewed and the responses varied without any consensus of opinion. The final segment of the production was an overall analysis and reflection held by each student. The results were remarkable. I gave all four students an A+. I kept the fifty-minute videotape for the purpose of showing it to the faculty at the next meeting, but someone got a hold of the tape and recorded over the first twenty minutes, thus ruining one of the best student-directed creative projects I have ever witnessed. After graduation, two of the students went to work on television production in Los Angeles for one of the major networks. The narrator of the project went into the broadcasting field and wrote me a letter from some Midwestern community where he became an anchor for a local news program. I never did find out what happened to the fourth person.

As in any student-oriented project, there are certain caveats that need to be addressed. On one occasion, I had some of my best students make a film utilizing the western genre. I didn't monitor their work and was satisfied to wait for the finished project. One of the student's mother was president of the PTA and enthusiastically told me how good the presentation was going to be. She even asked me for a copy of the videotape to show at the next PTA meeting. Apparently she previewed the video and thought that it was excellent. On the day the students gave their presentation to the class, I invited the administration to come in and see it. Thank God no one showed up! The video began with four male students urinating on a fence and it grew progressively worse. One of the students put two balloons in the front two pockets of his Levis and walked around through the whole film with them fully inflated. I watched about five minutes and demanded that they stop the video when one of the students was having sex with a ewe and the other males were lined up behind him. I didn't wait for the female roles to be shown. The class was in hysterics as I was sliding down my chair on to the floor in embarrassment. I confiscated the video, summarily destroyed it, and told the students that the presentation was unacceptable. The president of the PTA continued to inquire about when I was going to release the video for viewing by the group. I responded that it was not an appropriate film and tried to avoid any confrontation. The matter was dropped after I told the principal what I had seen on the tape. Thank God Augie was no longer around to challenge me and accuse me of denying the students "freedom of expression."

CHAPTER 12

Field Trips and Excursions

Field trips are one of the great educational advantages given to students in American schools. To take students out of the classroom and experience "the real world" is both rewarding and enriching. During election years, the American Government classes would divide up the classes and go out and canvas the entire Starr Valley area to find out how people would vote on both the candidates and issues on the ballots. We would make this an all-day affair by excusing the students from their regular classes and assigning them certain neighborhoods where they would go in two-person teams from house to house with the purpose of finding out how the general public feels about the candidates and issues. We used school busses to ferry groups throughout the valley. When the surveys were completed, we tallied the responses and made predictions on how the election would go. Some students were assigned to go to shopping centers and ask people to respond to questionnaires. To avoid duplication, students would ask each person if they had already been contacted regarding the survey. If people were unwilling to comment, students were required to respect their privacy and not be insistent. The first few times we did these surveys, the results were remarkably similar to the newspaper results after the election. However, there were always a few students who wouldn't do the surveys and make up answers while they took time off to do what they wanted. There were accusations by a few members of the community that students were engaging in illegal activities during these days, although none were ever substantiated. When the problem seemed to intensify, we cancelled future polling because the reliability of the findings became questionable. Most of the students who did the polling were responsible and took their tasks seriously. When we informed the classes that there were a few students who cheated on the results, there was an angry response and a willingness to expose and punish the cheaters. However, many of the faculty members were upset over not having the students being in their classes, and the administration tended to support their views thus bringing closure to the whole program.

Every May the school would suspend regular classes and take a week to engage in an alternative schedule. The first alternative schedule was called "pioneer week." During this week, the teachers and students would get involved in some activity that was not related to the regular curriculum. There would be classes on how to cook food the way it was done without any modern appliances, classes on how to ride horses, classes on western literature, and anything that was related to the lives of early pioneers. Teachers, administrators, and students would dress up in western garb during the week. Local ranchers and farmers would volunteer their time to come in and give talks about their livelihood. There were demonstrations by some of the ranchers on how to brand cattle, wrestle steers, and break-in wild horses.

During this week, I organized a field trip with some of the other teachers. We hired two busses and went up through the gold country to Empire Mine State Park outside of Nevada City, Donner Memorial State Park, and Virginia City, Nevada. On the third day, we returned to Starr Valley. The trip was so successful that it prompted me to set up an elective course the following Spring on the History of the American West with the stipulation that the course culminate with a week-long trip through the Sierras including the places we studied about during the semester.

There were no exams for the course. We read books on the West, saw films depicting the history of the West, and interviewed authors. Each student was required to do research on some part of Western history and give both a written and oral report to the class. For example, we read *Ordeal by Hunger* by George Stewart, saw the American Experience TV production of the tragedy of the Donner Party, and interviewed the author. George Stewart had retired from teaching at the University of California. I contacted him and asked him if he would be interested in being personally interviewed by some of my students. Three of them accompanied me to meet him and ask some questions raised by the class regarding his research. We audiotaped the interview and presented to the class his views. It was a great success! Inspired by his presentation, some students took the initiative to contact other authors. We read *The Gentle Tamers of the West* and *Bury My Heart at Wounded Knee* by Dee Brown. As part of their project requirements, a couple of students contacted him in Oklahoma and asked him if he would be willing to respond to a series of questions raised in class regarding his research. He complied by sending them two, two-hour audiotapes by responding to each question. The students were enthralled by the eagerness of each author to engage in this activity.

During the last week of May, weather permitting, we went on a five-day excursion through the Sierra Nevada Mountains. We started the week by going through the Gold Country, including the Empire Mine and Donner Memorial State Parks. We avoided Virginia City because it was too commercialized. Instead we spent a day going to the ghost town of Bodie, California, and would spend the last two days camping out at the group campground in Yosemite National Park before returning late Friday evening to Starr Valley. Before we arrived in Yosemite, we would stay overnight in high school gyms. Students were divided into food groups and each group was responsible for buying and properly storing their food. In every place we had rangers or local guides give the students lectures or tours. Students were required to keep photographic and accompanying written journals of each place and the presentations made. Most of the students who went on these tours stated that it was the highlight of their high school experiences. Periodically, when there are class reunions, former students will come up to me and express their thanks for organizing and leading these tours. However, not all these tours were problem free.

On one occasion we stayed at a high school in north Lake Tahoe. Because of a school function we weren't allowed to come to the school until after 9:00 PM. We had free access to Harrah's Auto Collection in nearby Sparks, Nevada, so we took the whole group to view approximately one thousand vehicles. The exhibit closed at 6:00 PM, so we let the students go in groups to eat in downtown Reno with the stipulation that no one would be allowed to go into the gambling casinos. The chaperones didn't have to monitor their actions in this regard because the casinos did the job for us. One of the casinos had some slot machines on the sidewalk outside of the main floor. I happened to be playing the machines when four of my female students came up to me stating, "Daddy, when are we going to have dinner? We have only eaten that one bag of crackers since yesterday!" There were two middle-aged women who were playing the slots next to me, and both gave me a look that "could kill." As the girls were trying to pull me away from the machines, I decided to play along and stated, "You could all use the lack of food as a sign of the need to diet!" Not one of them was fat! As we were engaging in this charade, I noticed that the women were loading their purses with their winnings and were wrapping the straps around their wrists with threatening gestures. I believe they were about to launch an offensive when one of the girls stated, "I think we better leave quickly!" Needless to say, we left quickly and got halfway down the block before we all broke out in laughter. Apparently, the women got a hold of the police department stating that there was a case of "child abuse." A patrol car stopped us as we were going across the street and asked if everything was all right citing the report they received from some caller. Since we were all laughing, they shook their heads, smiled and drove off.

One of the great lessons I've learned about chaperoning trips is the fact that if there is a problem it would always be brought to my attention by some of the students. I never needed to go out looking for trouble. On this same trip, two days later, one of the girls on the trip came up to me on the bus and said that the night we were in Reno, one of the other girls apparently dropped her drawers and mooned the crowd at a fast food eatery. I, then, decided to set an example to the group. We had stayed overnight at high school in the gold country, and the next morning we, as a group, went to a coffee shop for breakfast before heading off to Yosemite. While we were waiting for our breakfasts, a couple of deputy sheriffs from Amador County came in and sat at the table next to me. They were interested in why so many students had crowded the café. I had a long talk with them and told them about the trip and where we were going. I noticed that a couple of the girls were acting strange while I was talking to the officers. As we were departing, I got on the inner com and stated, "We will be taking a slight detour by the sheriff's office because there was a report of an indecent exposure by some high school girls in Reno, and there was photographic evidence of both the face and the 'exposure' perpetrated by the culprit, but they were sure that none of my group was involved!" The bus pulled over across the street from the sheriff's office and I had the whole group get out and line up on the sidewalk. A couple of deputy sheriffs were looking out the window with puzzled expressions. I noticed that one girl did not join the line up, and I found her in the back of the bus shaking like a leaf and with a petrified expression on her face. She said, "I did it! Will they arrest me? I am really sorry and won't do it again!" I couldn't keep a straight face and started laughing. One of the officers came out to ask if everything was all right, and I responded that we were only stretching our legs before departing for Yosemite. We didn't have any problems from that point on as the students were all laughing at the incident. The poor girl became known as "mooner," and even today at class reunions this story is told over again.

On another trip, I had a problem with two girls who decided to bring a case of twelve-ounce cans of beer. Each one was neatly wrapped up in aluminum foil and was kept out of sight in their sleeping bags. I knew the parents of one of the girls, and, as in every trip, I had the phone numbers of all the parents in case of an emergency. On this particular trip, I drove an SUV and the other teachers chaperoned the group on the bus. It was a Monday night and we were staying at a high school in north Lake Tahoe. The other chaperones and I had established 11:00 PM as the lights out curfew because we had to depart the next morning before 7:00 AM due to school starting at 8:00 AM. I had just settled down on my cot with a sleeping bag when one of the girls from the tour came up and said that the two who had brought the beer had stuffed their sleeping bags and snuck out to go to some party. This was about twelve midnight. I immediately told the other chaperones that I had to leave and find out where they went. For the next two hours, I searched every pizza parlor and eating establishment in the area. I drove through the quiet residential neighborhoods near the school listening for any signs of a party and found nothing but peace and quiet. I even went to the only gambling casino in the area but didn't find them. I returned to the high school and contacted the night janitor in order to use the phone. I called the parents, told them what had happened and stated that I would be sending them home by plane the next day. Before I got off the phone one of the other girls said that someone was knocking at the door in the rear of the gym. I investigated and found the two missing girls who were close to hyperthermia. I immediately got back on the phone and had the girls talk to their parents. Apparently they went out looking for a party that never materialized. They spent the next four hours walking around the school trying to find a way to sneak back in. They had left their coats stuffed in their sleeping bags and went out into the cold night with short-sleeved shirts and shorts. The temperature at night was hovering around 38°F. I barely got one hour sleep that night. The next day I had one of the other chaperones drive the girls to the airport and get them squared away. The girls tried to sneak the case of beer through the metal detector setting off the alarm. The beer was returned to us by the chaperone and was appropriately disposed of. When we returned to Starr Valley, the girls were anticipating that we had kept the beer and were expecting to retrieve it. I didn't pursue any disciplinary action against the girls because they suffered enough. I did inform the parents about what happened including the beer episode. They were grateful that I didn't take further action and stated that we earned the beers.

Not all of the six trips that we took were marred with problems. If students brought liquor on any of the trips, they were extremely discreet about it. I can usually tell by the behavior of the students if something was amiss, and except for a few questionable times, there were no problems. After the trip was over, I always asked some of the most trusted students in the class if they observed any drinking or partying going on, and with one exception, the responses were all negative. In fact, most of the students who were on the tours were excellent and well-behaved. A couple of boys who took one of the tours had never been to Yosemite and were enthralled with the valley and all the hiking trails. One of them went to college and majored in forestry. The last time I saw him he was one of the chief rangers in Yosemite National Park and was being interviewed on national television regarding a fire that had been out of control in one of the remote areas of the park.

One of the requirements to get into Yosemite Park without paying the fee was to arrange for some program within the Park. Since the primary purpose of our tour was to engage in some sort of enrichment program associated with the History of the American West, I made prior arrangements with the Park Service to have lectures or demonstrations conducted by the Park staff. In some cases, rangers would lecture about the pioneers who first came to the valley and what their lives were like, or they would provide Native American spokesmen who talked about the valley prior to the arrival of white man. On one occasion we had a graduate student from UC Berkeley, named Mark, who was working for the Park Service for the summer. He was trying to finish his Ph. D. in Cultural Anthropology and was earning extra money by conducting lectures and demonstrations dealing with the lives of the Native Americans who once inhabited the valley floor. He began by asking the students where they were from. When they responded, "Starr Valley," he lost his temper and went into a tirade against the banks and local government of Starr Valley. I couldn't believe this diatribe and almost immediately dismissed the students from this morning's obligation to hear his presentation. I interrupted him and asked why he was so antagonistic toward the students and their hometown. He calmed down and apologized for his outburst while relating the reasons for his animosity. Apparently he was doing research in Starr Valley regarding a burial ground, which was rich with artifacts of the Native Americans who resided in the valley for centuries. The land where the research was being conducted was owned by a bank, which was going to build a branch over the digs. He requested a three-year delay so that his team of anthropologists could finish their work. When the bank denied him his request, he went to the city council with a prepared presentation justifying the delay and the importance of his work. Apparently, the city council was more interested in gaining the tax dollars from the bank project and rejected his appeal. He went to the headquarters of the bank in San Francisco and pleaded with the CEO with the same presentation he gave to the city council. The CEO listened politely and said he would discuss his proposal with the board of directors. Two weeks later, he received a letter allowing him to conduct his research until spring when they would start the building process. He received the letter in February and was given until the end of April to finish his research. That winter was one of the wettest on record, and because of the muddy conditions, Mark and his team couldn't do much work. He repeated his appeal to both the Starr Valley city council and the bank but was rejected by both. He had to alter his entire research and start over in another part of California.

The students who remained to listen to him wrote a group letter to both the bank and the city council supporting Mark's project but it was too late.

While we were in Yosemite, we established strict rules regarding where students went. All students had to go in teams of at least two, had to sign out giving their destination, and sign back in at least one hour before dark. The students organized their meals according to the food groups and all were required to join a group before the tour began. On one occasion, I had a group of students who brought steaks and kept them on dry ice until we got to the camp ground. A couple of them brought candles and a tablecloth. For that night, they dined by candlelight, with steaks, French-fried potatoes, and tossed salad purchased at the village store. The chaperones were all impressed with the planning and presentation that went into their dinner. The next year, the food groups established a tradition of trying to out do each other with regard to what they ate and how they would set the tables. The one exceptional case of drinking occurred when some students brought a bottle of red wine to have with dinner. They didn't try to open it until after we had left for dinner; however, one of the chaperones confiscated it prior to them opening it. While we were in Yosemite, some of the chaperones usually went to the Lodge for dinner after we had checked everyone in. It was our time to get away and relax. There was always at least one chaperone who stayed behind, and that was usually determined by the degree of fatigue from the day's hikes. By the time we returned to the camp and took roll, three quarters of the students were sleeping out of sheer exhaustion. The students who brought the bottle of wine apologized and asked to be not be suspended from school upon returning from the trip. I had to report it to the parents and the school administration. They were assigned to Saturday detail and were reprimanded by their parents.

In Yosemite Valley, we stayed at the group camp ground and had some problems with bears. All the students were warned not to leave any food around and secure all in the bear-proof containers strategically located through out the campground. One afternoon one of the students, named Fred, who had been hiking with the others was very tired and was lying down on his sleeping bag outside of his tent. Unfortunately, he had been eating a bag of potato chips and left it by the side of his air mattress. One of the other students who was taking a nap awakened and saw a bear straddling him while eating the leftovers. No one made any noise fearing that the sleeping student would awaken and confront the bear. I happen to be returning from a hike and the other students came running up to me explaining the situation. I told them not to make any noise and I sent two of them to find the rangers as quickly as they could. I organized a team of the five remaining and we got all the noisiest utensils and were prepared to bang them to frighten away the bear in case Fred awoke. Luckily, the bear had finished eating the potato chips and licked Fred's face. Fred rolled over without awakening and the bear decided to wander off. By the time the rangers arrived, the bear was gone, and Fred was starting to wake up. The rangers stated that our strategy was the best defense in case any problems ensued. When Fred was awake we told him what happened, and he thought we were crazy. To this day, I don't believe that Fred accepted what we told him. I did make an announcement to the group that even in daylight bears can wander into camps looking for food. The warning was heeded!

On another occasion, we had two other groups on each side of our camping area. One was from South Central Los Angeles and the other from Beverly Hills. The first group were all Afro-American junior high school students and were the best behaved and best led groups of students I have ever encountered. They quietly woke up early in the morning and were gone on some venture all day. At night they all quietly went to bed in order to get up early for the next day's excursions. Their campground was spotless and well maintained. I commented to their counselors how it was a pleasure to have them near and apologized for any noise made by our group while they were trying to sleep. One of the counselors stated that they were so tired when the returned to camp that they ate their dinners early and were sound asleep before the sun had fully set. On the other side were the most obnoxious group of teenagers I have ever encountered. I didn't notice any chaperones from this group and assumed that they were all on their own. On the first night, the smell of marijuana was so strong it almost made our campground high. I was proud of our kids because they had the same impressions of the group that I did. A couple of our kids came to me and said that some of their group tried to sell "pot" to our kids but were rejected. A couple of our boys were ready to go over and "punch out" the more obnoxious members of the group. There was very little interaction between our group and the "spoiled brats" as they were labeled by our group until the second night when two hysterical girls came running into our camp demanding that I come over and rescue one of the boys who was trapped in the bathroom by a bear. I told them that they needed to contact the rangers and tell the boy to remain calm. I heard the boy screaming at the top of his lungs and decided to investigate. Two of the counselors from the junior high group also heard the screaming and we all went over to see what we could do. The boy was hysterical and demanded that we chase away the bear. The Beverly Hills group were now all screaming at us. I lost my temper and told them to all go back to their tents and shut up. The bear was one of the largest bears I have ever seen, and it decided to climb on top of the roof of the toilet facility. While we were telling the boy in the bathroom to remain calm and stop screaming, one of the girls started swearing at me demanding that I rush after the bear and chase it away. When I didn't respond to her commands, she started to attack me with her fists, and our female chaperone stepped in to restrain her. I came very close to slapping the girl across the face. About that time, some rangers came on the scene and the wrath of the group was focused toward them. We left the scene shortly afterward as the rangers managed to chase the bear away. The rangers, seeing the attitudes and behavior of the group along with the mess, informed them that they had to vacate the premises the next morning or school busses would be brought in to take the whole group to some detention facility in Mariposa. The next morning they were gone but the trash and mess that was left behind was appalling. I talked to one of the rangers the next morning who came to check on their departure, and he said that they had contracted the campground for seven days and were forced out after two. After they were gone, a work crew was pulled off another job to clean up the mess. Apparently, it was an all day job.

Bodie, California, is one of the best preserved "ghost towns" in the American West. It is approximately eleven miles off highway 395 on the eastern slope of the Sierra Nevada Mountains near Mono Lake. When we were there in the 1970s, there were seven miles of paved roads and four miles of dirt roads leading up to the site. The whole permanent population consists of two rangers and their families who watch over this state historic park the entire year. During the summer months hundreds of tourists visit the site to wander around the buildings, take pictures, and generally try to capture the historic atmosphere. The town was part of a second gold rush during the latter part of the nineteenth and early twentieth centuries. The last miners left shortly before World War II and the State of California made it into a State historic site sometime after the war was over. The rangers say that the whole town is in a state of "arrested decay" which apparently means that all efforts were being made to preserve the historic integrity of the area without adding any new buildings or tourist amenities. There were public bathrooms and water fountains but no eating establishments. Next to Yosemite, the students enjoyed visiting this area the most. On one occasion, a student who was hiking up on one of the hills had found a rock with gold streaks in it. We were told by the rangers not to take anything away from the area, but the girl who found the rock decided to hide it in her backpack and say nothing. I was told by the girl on the last day of school that she went to an assay office after returning home and had the rock examined. It apparently had a large core of gold that wasn't seen until the rock was crushed. I told the girl that she violated the law and created a potential problem for future group visitations. The girl, acting out of a sense of guilt, put all the contents of the rock into a box and sent it to the state park service with a letter of apology. During the summer, she received a letter of gratitude from the director of the state park system with a lifetime pass to any state park within California. I also received a letter of commendation and certificate which allowed our trip free access to any state park in California without having to prove that our group was on an accredited, student-educational tour. Unfortunately, that was the last year we took this tour because the school district decided to cancel alternative schedule week because it conflicted with State-mandated testing.

CHAPTER 13

Expect the Unexpected

One of the basic adages about education is to always "expect the unexpected!" Throughout my career, I have encountered incidents that I was unprepared to handle, and it always led to "second guessing." How could I have handled the situation better? During my first year of teaching, I had a couple of experiences that underscored the problem. On one occasion, I was overseeing a research project in the library when one of my students, a very attractive girl named Kitty, came up to me to ask for my advice on a personal matter. I assumed that it had something to do with her research, and I directed her to the conference room. When we went into the room, I noticed that all her friends were at one table with their eyes glued to us and were whispering to each other. Kitty began, "My boyfriend wants to have sex with me, what should I do?" I couldn't speak for about two minutes, trying to conjure up a response. I replied, "Why are you asking me?" Her response was that I was young and probably understood her dilemma better than anyone on the faculty. I got an inkling that this was a possible "set up" concocted by the group of girls seeking to embarrass me. Before answering her, I looked out the window and all her girlfriends immediately focused on the books they were supposed to be reading. I should have dismissed the whole inquiry by stating that it was an inappropriate question and had no relevance to her assigned task, but I decided to discuss the pros and cons of her "dilemma." However, she began by asking questions about my personal life, and the whole focus of her questions were directed toward me. After about fifteen minutes of her trying to pry into the intimate nature of my life, it finally dawned on me that the real reason we were in the conference room had nothing to do with her "dilemma." I avoided responding to any of her personal questions and tried to be as objective as possible dealing with her "problem," but she persisted. My embarrassment must have been very evident because she batted her blue eyes and in a flirtatious manner stated that "I was cute when I blushed!" Fortunately, the school bell rang ending the period. After I regained my composure, I went straight to the dean of girls and told her what happened. She laughed and said that this was annual ritual among senior girls seeking to embarrass new male teachers.

Another time, I was overseeing a library assignment when another girl, named Flo, came up to me asking for some advice. Because of my last experience, I was leery of her intentions and scanned the room, looking for possible co-conspirators. There was no one paying any attention to either one of us, so I asked her what she wanted. Flo was not very intelligent and wasn't particularly attractive. She didn't seem to have any close friends in my class. Apparently over the weekend, she met some guy at a party, and within fifteen minutes, after they met, he presented her with a wedding ring and proposed to her. She was wearing the ring during our conference. She said it was a real diamond, but even with my glasses on, it was no larger than the sharp end of a pin. She asked me if she did the right thing accepting it. I am not a marriage counselor and have no inclinations toward being one, but I couldn't resist asking her a series of personal questions regarding her encounter. Her responses were very unsatisfactory: First, she did not know his last name and assumed his first name was Ernie. Second, he got her address and phone number but didn't give out his. Third, she didn't tell her parents because "they wouldn't understand!" I thought that this could best be handled by her counselor and made that suggestion. She said that she didn't get along with her counselor and was unwilling to deal with any administrators. My advice to her was to contact "Ernie," break it off, and return the ring (or whatever it was). She said that she had no way of contacting him and then broke down crying. I was very sympathetic with her but couldn't get involved. When class ended, I immediately went to the dean of girls because Flo seemed very depressed. Luckily, I made the right decision because the girl attempted suicide that afternoon after skipping the rest of her classes. The dean of girls followed through with my report and her parents discovered that she had purposely taken an overdose of sleeping pills and found her unconscious in her bedroom. After she was rushed to the emergency room for treatment and recovery, the staff doctor said that they caught her in time, but she would have some permanent damage to some of her vital organs. She dropped out of high school and went through some rehabilitation program provided by the county. I never heard from her again and never did find out what happened to her.

When I was in my last year of coaching swimming, I had a young man named Jay who was an excellent swimmer and was one of the major reasons we won the league championship that season. However, there was an "unexpected" incident that was both very embarrassing and humorous. The last swim meet of the season is what is called the sectional meet. After all the dual meets and the league finals, qualifiers are eligible to compete in this two-day meet. There were approximately four different sectional meets through out California and some of the best swimmers in the world compete for medals and ribbons. The meet was held in a coastal town approximately one hundred miles from Starr Valley. The first day's competition included the trial heats where the competition is narrowed and only the fastest times qualify for the next day's finals. It was an all-day affair as different swimmers from high schools all over the section wait until they are called to compete. The weather was very cold that day, and virtually every swimmer brought a sleeping bag with him in order to keep warm while waiting for his turn. Jay was one of those swimmers who brought his girlfriend along to "keep him warm"! Apparently he wasn't keeping track of when his turn was coming, and he and his girlfriend became too amorous. When the loud speaker announced his name, Sam and I couldn't find him. He showed up just in time as the judges were ready to disqualify him. Unfortunately, he was wearing his Speedo swimsuit and had been sexually aroused. When he got up on the blocks, he had a towel wrapped around him and was bending over when the starter stated that he had to leave the towel and stand up straight. The whole pool area suddenly woke up and an uproar ensued. The more the people laughed, the more the protuberance hardened. One of the coaches yelled in jest that it was "illegal to have a rudder in the water." Another stated that his appearance gave a whole new meaning to the term "heat." Sam, who was always quick in responses, stated that there would been a greater complaint if Jay had swum the backstroke. He said, "You coaches would complain that he was using an illegal snorkel!" Poor Jay was turning red and his girlfriend had covered her head with the sleeping bag. I didn't see her the rest of the day. Jay did win his heat and qualified for the next day's finals where he placed in the top five finishers. His girlfriend did not show up for the finals.

Joselyn was a young lady that I had in my US History class in the 1980s. She was a very attractive, well-groomed, and immaculately dressed young lady who looked like she stepped out of *Seventeen* magazine. She always wore a dress or a skirt and blouse combination to class every day. I thought that she must have modeled after school for some high-end clothing store but never asked. She was a delight to have in class as she was a very good student, attentive, and well-behaved. She had a circle of friends who were all very pleasant, good students, and took their class work very seriously. None of them would fit into the current label of being a "hotty." None of these girls seemed to have serious boyfriends, although they seemed very friendly toward the brighter boys in the class. I noticed that none of Joselyn's friends wore the same type of clothing. In fact, they seemed be part of the jeans and sweatshirt crowd, and Joselyn looked out of place when they hung out together. I had met her parents on a couple of occasions, and they were very nice and supportive of the school and my teaching style. I did notice that both of them were always well groomed and in tune with the current adult fashion trends. Joselyn's mother wrote me a very nice note at the end of the first semester explaining how much her daughter liked history and my style of teaching. This particular class was one of the most enjoyable groups of students I have ever had during my career; there were no discipline problems and everyone took their work seriously.

Joselyn's class came after lunch time and usually students suffer from a "sugar high" in the afternoon classes, but this group was different; every one of them came into class and began working with little or no prompting from me. On one particular day during the spring semester, I had another "unexpected" incident. The weather was warm and all the students were spread out all over campus eating their lunches when the bell sounded to go to class. I remember sitting at a desk in front of the class when Joselyn came into class with tears in her eyes. I didn't say anything to her, but I noticed that she was upset over something. I was giving the students a workday where they could quietly do their assignments or work on some other class work. About ten minutes into the class, Joselyn came up to me, crying and saying that she was hurting from a bee sting suffered during lunch. Without thinking, I asked where she was stung. She lifted up her skirt and showed me where the bee had stung her. She had been stung in the most "intimate" part of her anatomy, which she didn't try to conceal. I immediately sent her to the nurse for treatment. She thanked me and left the class. It must have taken me approximately one minute to realize the magnitude of what just happened. I immediately surveyed the classroom to see how many students had noticed. There was not one response! Usually in a situation like this, most students would be giggling or whispering. I came to the conclusion that not one student out of a class of thirty-three witnessed the incident. Joselyn's friends who were in the class weren't sitting near her and were completely absorbed into their work. I did not feel that it was appropriate to bring up the matter to anyone unless the nurse, counselor, or administrator launched an inquiry. None was forthcoming! The next day, Joselyn came to class and didn't say a thing about what she did and acted as though nothing ever happened. I hesitated to ask her about the sting and didn't make any comment.

As she was leaving class, she thanked me for sending her to the nurse, and that was it! In retrospect, I don't believe that she thought about nor saw any ramifications in what she did. I thought about informing an administrator and especially her counselor but decided to "let sleeping dogs lie" and that was it.

CHAPTER 14

Teaching Has Its Rewards

I have had some remarkable students in my classes during the forty-five years of teaching. One became a congressman from the State of California, one became a billionaire commercial property developer, others became prominent in medicine, law, and other professional occupations. Coming from Starr Valley, they all had advantages that most urban students from lower-income brackets did not have. Very few of my students did not go to college. During my tenure as a full-time teacher, I served in various district committees that oversaw the academic development and achievement of students who went on to college and became successful both academically and professionally. On one occasion, I had to contact various colleges regarding the achievements of our graduates and where they stood in comparison with students from other high schools through out the state. We were ranked in the top 10 percent of all the schools in California with regard to college preparation and achievement. I always regarded this with a sense of pride and fulfillment. Perhaps this, more than anything else, kept me in education for thirty-six years of full-time teaching and nine additional years of teaching only the Advanced Placement United States History class. I always felt blessed that I was given the opportunity to deal with a remarkable number of high-quality students.

One of the questions that always comes up in discussion and reflection when dealing with students is, "Is there any one student who for some reason stands out or was uniquely memorable in your career?" This is always a very difficult question to answer because of the ten thousand or more students that I have encountered. Some were outstanding scholars and great leaders both in school and in their careers. There was one student that I had in the 1970s who probably more than any of the others was uniquely memorable.

Her name was Nadeen.

On the first day of school, I always keep two desks near the entrance to the class room for students who, for whatever reason, come late to class. On this particular day, a young lady who looked like she stepped out of a Norman Rockwell painting came into class five minutes late. I noticed that she was walking very slowly and had some difficulty in getting into her seat. She was very polite and apologized for coming in late. I noticed that the whole class focused on her without a word being spoken. In the next few days, the same scene was reenacted. I didn't say any thing to her except to tell her to try to make it to class on time. I noticed that on the next few days she brought a cane with her to class. During one of my breaks, I went to her counselor to find out about the nature of her problem. Her counselor looked at me for a few seconds without responding and then her eyes teared up. It seemed that Nadeen was dying of bone cancer and had approximately three or four months left to live. I asked her why she came to school with so little time left. Apparently her parents wanted to take her out of school and take her on a European tour, but Nadeen insisted that she wanted to go to school and be with her friends. For the next week, she came to class with a walker and in a month was in a wheelchair. The reason for her being the most memorable was her discussion and insight during class discussions. After a couple of weeks, she came up to me and asked if she could bring her lunch and have continued discussions with me during the Friday noon hour. I, of course, was willing to sit down and discuss any of the issues that prompted her curiosity. One of the subjects that I carefully avoided was religion. This became a regular Friday ritual, and I looked forward to our discussion. The most remarkable part of our meetings was the maturity and wisdom that she demonstrated. On many occasions, some of her closest friends would join us. Our discussions focused on human motivation, war, philosophy, and many other esoteric issues that are not normally discussed in class.

After the Christmas break, there are usually two weeks of class before final exams. This time is usually very hectic because all the teachers are busy preparing exams and compiling grades for the end of the semester. I had Nadeen in class just before the lunch break, which meant that she could just stay in class for our discussions. Unfortunately, the last Friday before finals I was very busy and had to cancel our noon meeting. I remember that day for another reason. She came to class with a radiance that I have never seen on a human being. She seemed to glow. I commented to her at the beginning of class by asking her if she was using a new type of makeup. She blushed and was perplexed by the question, so I apologized. I asked my student aide if she say anything different about Nadeen's appearance and she said, "No, why?" I couldn't answer.

That afternoon, one of Nadeen's friends came up to me and made the same observation. We couldn't figure out why she looked so different. After school, I was discussing with some of her other teachers if they had noticed anything different about her, and all replied that they hadn't. On Monday morning, I received a note in my box that Nadeen had passed away on Sunday morning in her sleep. Needless to say, I became very emotional and couldn't function very well during that day. Her parents had a very private funeral for members of the family only. The following week, there was a school memorial service for her and most of her classmates attended. I received a very nice letter from her mother regarding how much she enjoyed my class and especially our noon discussions. Two years later, I had her younger and healthier sister in my class. During our "back to school" night, Nadeen's parents came up to me and told me what a great influence I had on her during the last few months of her life. I was very emotionally touched by this accolade and have never forgotten the bravery and insight that she demonstrated during the brief time that I knew her. Upon careful reflection, I believe that dealing with people like Nadeen and her family makes my profession one of the greatest and most rewarding of them all.

CHAPTER 15

Advanced Placement or
Advanced Pain?

I have always been asked by former students how today's students are different from past classes in terms of behavior, achievement, motivation, etc. The question predisposes that their class was better and teenagers to day are incorrigible and have more problems than the older generation. I have always stated, in response, that teenagers are the same regardless of the generational differences. The conditions change, but their actions and behavior are basically the same. It is difficult to measure the achievement levels of today's teenagers from their predecessors in terms of their academic pursuits, responses to adversity, initiative, and leadership. There will always be high achievers and low achievers with the majority in the middle. Students in the advanced placement classes are usually in the top category, but in the last few years, I have noticed that there is a growing trend in today's schools to encourage all students to take AP classes. I believe that this is a product of the demands colleges impose on all incoming students. Unfortunately, not all students who take AP classes are prepared to take on the rigorous demands that these classes require. Parents, today, seem to assume that their children are academically motivated enough to meet the challenges, and when they fail to measure up to the standards of these classes, it is everyone else's fault but their own progeny.

When I first started teaching Advanced Placement United States History, I had difficulty trying to establish some criteria to judge whether students would be able to handle the rigors and demands of the course work. Unfortunately, I had no guidance from the school or the district administrations on what would be an acceptable test or assessment instrument whereby I could "weed out" students who wouldn't be able to compete. I had to make up exams and writing proficiency exercises to make the proper judgment. This was a daunting task because every time I came up with a measurable instrument the question of fairness and applicability prompted me to evaluate and reevaluate the process. For the first ten years that I taught the class, the administration refused to open up additional classes and many social studies teachers felt that their best students were being taken out of their classes. Their complaints were certainly valid, but when I pushed for more classes, none of them wanted any part of the changes. It wasn't until colleges mandated that students take advanced placement classes that we were able to make the proper changes.

CHAPTER 16

Conclusions

After forty-five years of teaching, I felt that it was time to retire. In writing these memoirs, I have left a lot of my experiences and perceptions out of this text and have tried to be both entertaining and informative. As the reader has surmised, I have been very fortunate in my education experiences. In retrospect, I believe that I chose the best profession to accomplish my goals in life.

With regard to all my colleagues and administrators, I feel that, with a few noted exceptions, there was little or no conflict. Although I took advanced courses in college to increase my pay, keep abreast of the times, and to obtain an administrative credential, I am glad that I did not pursue the administrative course for my career. One year I was given the opportunity to be a quasi-administrator by teaching two regular history classes, a leadership class, and serving two periods as director of student activities. Unfortunately, almost every night was taken up with some extracurricular activity.

Teaching the leadership class was a challenge because there was no curricular standards to use as a basis for instruction. The problem was further complicated because all the members of the spirit squads were in the class and to a person were more interested in putting on makeup, discussing boys, and making signs for upcoming activities. In the past, there was no instruction given to these students, and they pretty well did what they wanted. There was an uproar when I demanded a project, which required research in order to earn a grade. They were required to interview and record responses from civic leaders, business leaders, and others who have been involved in leading and motivating groups to accomplish their assigned goals. The results varied and were interesting. Each person was required to give some sort of visual presentation to the class as a whole in addition to submitting a written project.

The results were predictable regarding both business and civic leaders and the information and advice were quite valuable. One of the students had an unusual interview with a gang boss who happened to be in jail at the time. The student's father was a corrections officer who was part of a rehabilitation program in the county prison system. The gang leader's responses were recorded on video tape and the student presented them to the class. It was the most interesting and provocative interview and captured the attention of the whole class. Unfortunately, the gang leader's defense attorney had the tape confiscated before I could show it to the whole faculty. From what I remember, he had some good advice regarding how to avoid pitfalls in leading a group of people especially regarding "what not to do!" After one year as director of student activities, I resigned and went back to full-time teaching. There are some advantages of being a school administrator, but overall, there are few rewards dealing with faculty, parents, and students. Dealing with various forms of conflict, the long hours, and the politics involved were not what I envisioned to be a worthwhile career.

Over the years, I have established a good rapport with the parents of my students and looked forward to parent-night encounters. In our district "back to school" night meetings were too short, and in the last few years, I opted to set up my own night to meet with the parents. This usually lasted an hour, and I felt it was worthwhile. So did the parents. Unfortunately, I was criticized by my colleagues for establishing a potential precedent for future parent-teacher meetings.

However, this has never come to pass. The biggest problem with high school parent meetings was which parents came to the meetings. One year I taught a "developmental" class for students who were not doing well in the regular classes. During "back to school" night, not one parent showed up. For the advanced placement courses, there was standing room only. In the former class, it should have been mandatory that parents came to find out about the problems their students faced. There were parent conferences called during the regular school day to deal with individual problems, but as a teacher, I was disappointed with the results.

During the forty-five years of teaching, I believe that there were only a handful of students that I disliked, but they invariably transferred out of my classes after a short time. It was the interactions that took place both in class and outside of class that I have always cherished and kept me in education all these years.

About the Author

Lee Wildes taught, coached, and directed programs during 45 years of teaching high school in a suburban high school in California. He has taught Advanced Placement United States History, American Government and courses in European, Asian, Afro-American, and the History of the American West. He has worked for the College Board and Educational Testing Service during much of the time. After retirement he has been active in foundation scholarship programs for deserving students.

CPSIA information can be obtained
at www.ICGtesting.com
Printed in the USA
FSOW01n0451050815
9406FS